HISTORICAL RECORDS OF THE
20th (Duke of Cambridge's Own) INFANTRY
BROWNLOW'S PUNJABIS

MAJOR-GENERAL L. C. DUNSTERVILLE, C.B., C.S.I.

HISTORICAL RECORDS

OF THE

20TH (DUKE OF CAMBRIDGE'S OWN)

INFANTRY

BROWNLOW'S PUNJABIS

1908–1922

The Naval & Military Press Ltd

❖

Reproduced by kind permission of the Central Library,
Royal Military Academy, Sandhurst

Published by

The Naval & Military Press Ltd

Unit 10, Ridgewood Industrial Park,

Uckfield, East Sussex,

TN22 5QE England

Tel: +44 (0) 1825 749494

Fax: +44 (0) 1825 765701

www.naval–military-press.com

© The Naval & Military Press Ltd 2005

CONTENTS

APPENDICES

LIST OF ILLUSTRATIONS

LIST OF MAPS

HISTORICAL RECORDS OF THE
20TH (D.C.O.) INFANTRY

THE first volume of the Historical Records of the regiment carried us up to March, 1907, when celebrations in honour of the fiftieth anniversary of the raising of the regiment were held at Dera Ismail Khan.

In March, 1904, the death occurred of H.H. The Duke of Cambridge, Colonel-in-Chief of the regiment.

In June, 1904, General Sir Charles H. Brownlow, G.C.B., was appointed Colonel of the regiment. On 10th July, 1908, General Sir Charles Brownlow was promoted to the rank of Field-Marshal. In response to a telegram of congratulations from the regiment, Sir Charles Brownlow replied : " Salutations and thanks to regiment for honours due to their good conduct in the field."

In January, 1909, the regiment marched from Dera Ismail Khan to Jhelum, arriving there on 5th February.

In 1911 Subadar Major Ali Khan (Khambar Khel Afridi) proceeded to England with the Indian contingent, which took part in the coronation of His Majesty King George V.

In January, 1914, Lieutenant-Colonel C. Rattray (from the 26th Punjabis) succeeded Colonel L. C. Dunsterville as Commandant of the regiment.

In February, 1914, the regiment moved from Jhelum to Poona, moving by rail as far as Niphad (close to Nasik) and thence by route march.

In 1912 Subadars Saleh Khan and Diyal Singh were

admitted to the 2nd Class of the Order of British India, and in 1914 Subadars Moti and Unkar Singh received the same honour.

The Great War, 1914

At the outbreak of the Great War, on 4th August, 1914, the regiment was stationed at Poona, under the command of Lieutenant-Colonel C. Rattray. Four British officers— i.e. Major R. Ducat, Captains H. C. Rome, C. C. Stewart and Captain C. H. Graham, I.M.S.—were on leave in England. The usual percentage of Indian ranks were on leave and furlough, all of them in Northern India ; many of the trans-frontier men were in most inaccessible localities across the frontier. On 10th August all officers were recalled from leave, and two days later all Indian ranks were also recalled and the reservists embodied. Mobilization orders were received on the night of 14th/15th August. These orders were for I.E.F. " B "—that is, for operations in East Africa.

Poona is so far from the regimental recruiting areas that considerable delay in assembling the regiment was anticipated. But it was only one week from the time that the recalling order was despatched when the first of the furlough men—a Dogra—rejoined. The Sikhs began to arrive the next day, the 20th, and were quickly followed by the Cis-frontier Pathans. This was extraordinarily rapid work. The trans-frontier men were of course longer in rejoining, having been summoned from such remote localities, and it was not until 8th September that the first of them reported. On 5th September one hundred and four reservists joined from Lahore, and the same day Major Ducat, Captain Stewart and Captain Graham, I.M.S., rejoined from leave ex-India. Captain H. C. Rome, who was also in England, was retained for duty. This gallant officer was later attached to the Indian troops in France, and was killed at Givenchy La Basse on 20th December, 1914, while with

BRITISH AND INDIAN OFFICERS
1913

the 129th Baluchis. On 1st September, at 5.0 p.m., orders had been received changing the destination of the regiment from I.E.F.B.—East Africa—to I.E.F.A.—i.e. France. It was then supposed that the regiment would leave on the 7th or 8th of the month. The actual date of departure eventually proved to be a full month later.

The G.O.C. Southern Army inspected the 16th Infantry War Brigade, of which the regiment now formed a part, on 26th September.

On 10th October, after a month during which all ranks were in daily expectation of an immediate move, orders were received for the regiment to leave Poona, on Monday, 12th October. The loading and entraining were begun at Ghorpuri siding at 5 p.m. on the 11th, and the train left at 6 a.m. the next morning and arrived at Bombay docks at 4.30 p.m. the same day. The heat was intense. The regiment detrained quickly and efficiently and embarked immediately on board the S.S. *Umaria*. The ship remained in dock that night with the 20th D.C.O. Infantry and the 117th Mahrattas—who had already embarked—on board.

The following British and Indian officers proceeded on service with the regiment :—

Lieutenant-Colonel C. Rattray.

Major R. Ducat.

,,   W. M. Fordham.

,,   R. S. St. John.

Captain B. H. Finnis.

,,   P. H. McCleverty.

,,   E. C. Irwin.

,,   P. D. Saxton.

,,   C. M. Hawes (Adjt.).

,,   H. J. Daniell.

Lieutenant C. H. M. Churchill.

,,   C. T. Burn Murdoch.

Captain G. F. Graham, I.M.S.

Subadar Major Ali Khan.
Subadar Saleh Khan.
    ,,   Masin Khan.
    ,,   Mota Singh.
    ,,   Imat Khan.
    ,,   Ganda.
    ,,   Kala Singh.
Jemadar Khan.
    ,,   Sant Singh.
    ,,   Barhawan.
    ,,   Kapura.
    ,,   Mawaz Khan.
    ,,   Wali Khan.
    ,,   Jhanda Singh.

Also the following, who were promoted from Havildar to Jemadar on 14th August :—

Jemadar Amin Gul.
    ,,   Pala Singh.
    ,,   Kashmir Singh.
    ,,   Chakand.
    ,,   Udham Singh.

The following day—13th October—the S.S. *Umaria* left docks and anchored in the stream. At 1.30 p.m. on that day orders were received detailing the 16th Infantry Brigade for I.E.F.D., an unknown destination.

No country in the world has ever seen such a force sail from one of its dependencies as left Bombay Harbour at five o'clock in the afternoon of 16th October. The great fleet of three warships and forty-six transports steamed slowly out over a sea crimson and gold in the sunset. On board were troops of many different races, creeds and languages, the only thing they had in common being their loyalty to the Empire. It was a moving and inspiring sight. There were troops for three separate areas ; " A " for Europe, cavalry, R.A., and infantry ; " B," under the command of

Brigadier-General Aitken, for German East Africa, artillery, infantry and Imperial Service troops; " D," under Brigadier-General Delamain, for an unknown destination. Force D consisted of the Dorsetshire Regiment, 104th Wellesley's Rifles, 117th Mahratta Light Infantry, 20th D.C.O. Infantry, 22nd Company Sappers and Miners. The fleet proceeded at the economic speed of the slowest ship, 9½ knots, due west.

The *Umaria* under normal conditions is suited to carry only one battalion. There were no cabins for either British or Indian officers. Wooden compartments had been run up and electricity installed, but there were no fans available. The ship was so crowded that only 50 per cent. of the men could be on deck at one time, so arrangements had to be made to ensure each man getting up for air two or three times a day. The health of the troops remained good in spite of the trying conditions. At this time the men were still convinced that they were bound for Europe, and were, as they had been since the prospect of active service first opened out to them, very happy and keen. They remained cheery and contented through the hot stormy days that followed, but a great disappointment was in store for them. On the 19th at 11.0 a.m. the convoy was joined by H.M.S. *Ocean* from European waters, and at 12.45 p.m. the *Ocean* turned north-west followed by the first group of transports. It was very hard for all ranks, after having been detailed for Europe, to see the main convoy go off leaving them, bound for an unknown destination. The main theatre of the War was closed to them, and it was with bitter regret that they proceeded on what promised to be only minor operations. It was not until the next day that a signal was received from H.M.S. *Ocean* giving the destination of the 14th Brigade as the Bahrein Islands. Before arriving there, while approaching the Straits of Ormuz, the convoy was joined by the R.I.M.S. *Dalhousie*, escorting transports from Karachi. The passage up the Persian Gulf was very hot but quiet, and on the 23rd, at 2.30 p.m., the convoy anchored off Bahrein, about 2 miles out. Orders were received for the brigade to camp at Bahrein in readiness to proceed up the Shat-el-Arab in the event of Turkey becoming hostile.

A very trying week followed. Men, horses and mules were all feeling the effect of two weeks on board a vessel greatly overcrowded. The ships were anchored nearly 2 miles out and were prevented from going in closer by a sand bar. The heat and discomfort were intense, but it was not possible to land, as the coastal conditions were so unfavourable that it would have taken a week to re-embark, or even longer in the event of a shumal blowing. On the 25th orders had been received to weigh anchor the next day, but these orders were subsequently cancelled and the long days of waiting passed slowly.

The men of the regiment—Pathans, Sikhs and Dogras—had a most intelligent grasp of the situation. Their hearts had been set on fighting in Europe, and they openly said that they had little enthusiasm for the operations in which we were likely to take part. There were also discernible among the Pathans the first faint mutterings of religious antagonism. They stated their position with a good deal of justice. While they did not in any way approve of Turkish misrule, which they realized was possibly corrupt and under bad German domination, nevertheless they objected strongly to being employed against their co-religionists, Suni Mohammedans. The Sultan was the head of their religion, and as such to be venerated. Why could not they be sent to fight Germans, and some of the many Indian regiments recruited from Dogras, Sikhs, Rajputs, Gurkhas, etc., whose religious susceptibilities would in no way be affected, be detailed to carry on the campaign with Turkey ? It was an argument that could be answered only by the necessity of obeying orders cheerfully.

A little comic relief was introduced into these weary days by the men practising boat drill and rowing, which they began on the 27th and continued for some days. Transfrontier Pathans and Sikh cultivators are not usually adepts at aquatic sports, and an oar was an instrument quite new in their experience. The oars had a way of taking command of the situation, to the dismay of the sepoys and the despair of the British coxswains who were training these amateur crews. One man narrowly escaped being caught by a shark when some more than usually obstreperous oar had knocked him out of the boat. However, they finally acquired enough skill to ensure both their staying in the boat and the boat moving in the desired direction !

On Saturday, 31st October, the plan of operations for landing and capturing Fao was made known to British officers. The next day a disembarkation rehearsal was held in the morning. Orders were received to be ready to sail —also the composition of the covering party for any landing was revealed. This covering party was to be made up of the Dorsetshire Regiment and the 20th D.C.O. Infantry under command of Lieutenant-Colonel Rosher of the Dorsets.

At 6.30 a.m. on Monday, 24th November, the transports left Bahrein. At 2 p.m. the following message was received from Brigade Headquarters : " Please inform the troops that a state of war exists between England and Turkey. Ever since the beginning of the war between England and Germany, England has made every endeavour to maintain peace and uphold the ancient friendship with Turkey, but, urged on by German intrigue, Turkey has made successive acts of aggression and England is now forced to declare war. This force has been sent up the Gulf to safeguard our interests and protect friendly Arabs from Turkish attacks."

The following day arrangements were begun to prepare

the *Umaria* for protecting the 117th Mahrattas and one section 23rd Mountain Battery, R.G.A., while they covered landing operations. All the troops were fit and very happy at once more being on the move, with the prospect of real work close ahead. Everything available was used for making breastworks—ration boxes, boxes and tins of coal, bags of flour, dhal and rice, bales of compressed hay. Wind screens were folded and filled with coal, and the *Umaria* presented a very efficient state of defence. At 9 p.m. all the transports anchored close to H.M.S. *Ocean*, 20 miles from Fao, on a bright, cool moonlight night. The next day was passed quietly. Orders were received as to tows for the landing force. Major Ducat was to proceed on the first tow; Lieutenant-Colonel Rattray, Majors Fordham and St. John and Captain Hawes in the second tow. At 11.15 a.m. on Thursday, 5th November, H.M.S. *Ocean* signalled orders to get up steam and move forward as soon as possible. The transports started, the *Varela* leading, followed by the *Umaria*, and at 1.30 p.m. dropped anchor about 5 miles from Fao. The shore was just visible, flat and closely wooded, with Fao fort, a low mud structure, at the mouth of the Shat-el-Arab. Operation orders were received that evening for the attack the next day.

The Landing at Fao

On Friday, 6th November, at 10 a.m., His Majesty's Sloop *Odin* opened fire on Fao while the first party under Major Ducat were getting into their boats. The Turks returned the fire, for some three hundred rounds—a futile expenditure of ammunition, as they hit the *Odin* only twice and did no harm at all. Luckily the force holding Fao, which had been estimated at five hundred infantry and eight guns, bolted at once, as the carefully rehearsed landing operations were not very efficiently carried out. The tows were very long, the ropes kept slipping, and the last boat, which contained Captain Irwin and the Machine-Guns, was in imminent danger of capsizing, as it was immediately over the screw. The idea was that the boats were to be towed to a certain point fairly close to the bank, anchored there until all were ready and then turn left and row for the shore. Unfortunately the Indian Marine officer responsible for putting the boats into position for landing had forgotten that, just at the hour when the operation was to be carried out, the tide turned. The result was that the boats all swung around at anchor. The men, never very expert at oarsmanship, lost what little skill they had. Some boats landed, some were carried out to sea, some were driven to the Persian shore. However, no damage was done, the errant boats were collected by launches, and by three o'clock the regiment landed at Fao telegraph office. There were a few Turks there who disappeared. Fao fort was some distance to the south of the telegraph office. There was a wide belt of date palms along the river, and inland, to the west, open desert. The main body, consisting of the Dorsets, 20th Infantry, one section 30th Mountain Battery, one section 23rd Company Sappers and Miners and some marines from the *Ocean*, moved around the area to the west of the date plantation and bivouacked for the night some way from the fort, on a mud flat.

Next morning they went on to the fort, which they found had already been occupied by the Left Flank Guard, Maxim Guns, Scouts and D Company under Major Ducat. The troops had proceeded direct through the trees to the fort, which they had entered unopposed at 9.30 the previous evening, at once establishing visual communication with the *Varela*.

By 3 p.m. on the 7th the force was all re-embarked on the transports, which proceeded up-stream. At six in the evening, on anchoring, the *Umaria* was fired at from a Turkish custom house. The fire was at once silenced by our Maxim and Mountain Battery guns, and nothing further occurred during the night. The custom house was destroyed by a party of Sappers and Miners and 117th, who were unopposed, the next morning.

The Landing at Sanniya

The ships went forward, and at 2 p.m. the 104th Infantry, 20th Infantry, and 1/2nd Battalion of Dorsets landed at Sanniya, on the right bank of the Shat-el-Arab 2 miles above Abadan, to clear the country and protect transports from surprise. There was some desultory fighting, with a few casualties among the Turks. The next two days were spent in landing the whole of the brigade and in making an entrenched camp. The trees which, here as lower down the river, grew in a belt along the bank were cleared, entrenching was carried on and a perimeter camp constructed. No tents were allowed, and as it rained heavily and rations were short, there was a good deal of discomfort involved.

During the night of 10th/11th November accurate information was received from the Sheikh of Mohammerah that a large force of the enemy was advancing. Piquets were reinforced, and at 5.30 a.m. the force was attacked from the north and west. Four companies with six guns of the 23rd Mountain Battery moved out to turn the enemy out of a village and date plantation south-east of an old fort which was situated about half a mile west of the camp. The enemy were routed, but Major Ducat was mortally wounded while leading his men, Subadar Imat Khan was severely wounded, one man was killed and four men wounded in the same attack. Major Ducat was buried that afternoon in the date plantation south of the camp—a very lovable, gallant gentleman and a severe loss to the regiment. The Turks lost a considerable number. The hostile force was estimated at 1,500, but only about three hundred actually took part in the attack.

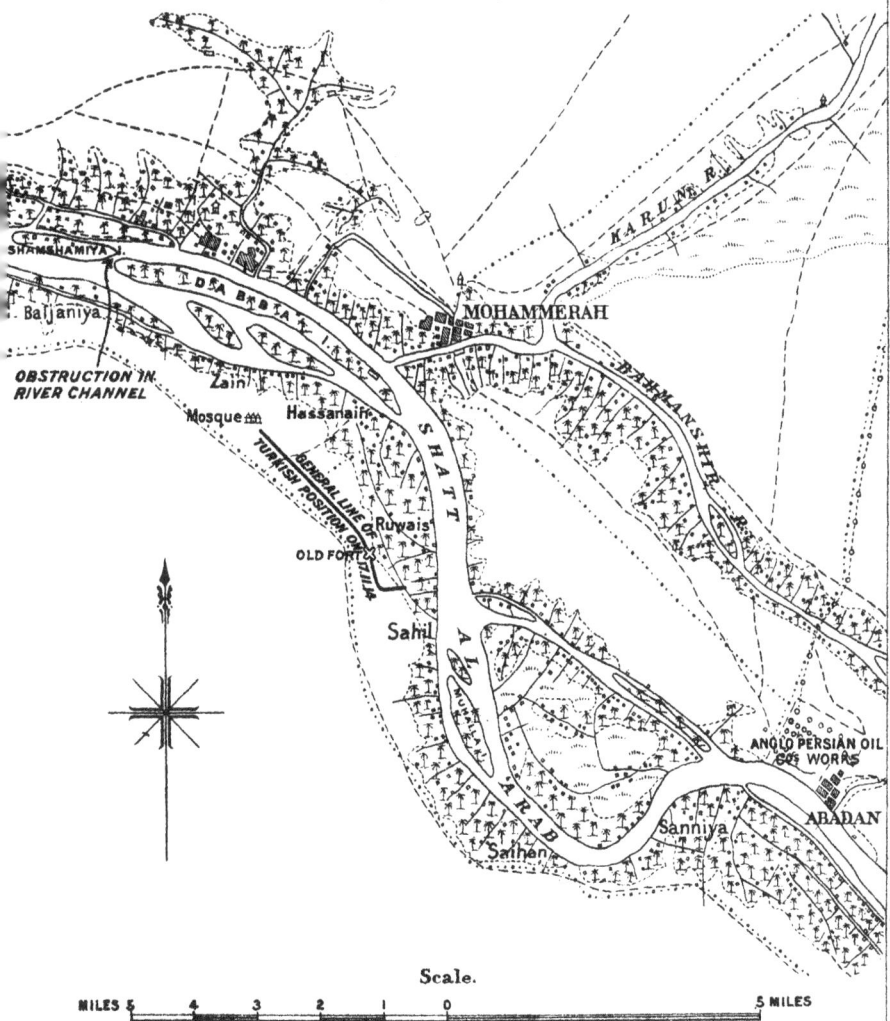

MAP Nº I.

to illustrate the landing at Sanniya and the action at Zain

SHAMSHAMIYA

Baljaniya

OBSTRUCTION IN
RIVER CHANNEL

Zain

Mosque

Hassanain

Ruwais

OLD FORT

Sahil

Saihan

Sanniya

DS'A B'A T A L

MOHAMMERAH

KARUN R.

BAHMANSHIR R.

S H A T T

TURKISH POSITION 19|11|14
GENERAL LINE OF

A L

A R A B

ANGLO PERSIAN OIL
Cº WORKS

ABADAN

Scale.

MILES 5   4   3   2   1   0   5 MILES

The next two days were spent in camp strengthening the perimeter and making roads. The rain continued. On the 14th, General Barrett, with the Divisional Staff of the 6th Division and six transports, joined the force. On the 15th the 16th Brigade made a reconnaissance and fought a successful action with the Turks about 3 miles to the north. The Turkish camp was captured, and a considerable amount of stores of all sorts, with few casualties. The regiment acted as reserve except H Company, which was sent to reinforce the 104th and became engaged in front of a strong village on the right. Bugler Surain Singh and Sepoy Bawa Singh set fire to the village with great gallantry. The conduct of the former was brought to the notice of Headquarters by the O.C. 104th.

The Action at Zain

On Tuesday, 17th November, the 6th Division left Sanniya at 6 a.m., and after a march of some 10 or 11 miles over wet alluvial soil, the enemy were discovered at Zain, nearly opposite Mohammerah. As far as the 16th Brigade was concerned, the attack was launched at 11 a.m., with the Dorsets on the right and the 20th Infantry on the left, supported by the 104th Rifles and the 48th Pioneers— against an old mud fort. Covered by the regimental scouts, the battalion advanced eastwards in two lines of double companies with a double company in local reserve, echeloned on the left—the distances and intervals 250 and 100 yards respectively. Owing to a severe rain-storm the ground was very heavy, and the scouts were unable, in spite of their superior pace, to precede the battalion by more than 200 or 300 yards. About 11.40 Captain Saxton, scout officer (by this time seriously wounded), reported enemy infantry in a trench north-west of the old fort and some thousand yards west of the date groves, with a gun and cavalry on the edge of the wood south-west of the fort. The advance continued under shrapnel fire until about noon, when the enemy suddenly opened heavy rifle-fire from a trench about 800 yards to the east, against the front of the battalion and from the wood to the south-east against the right. It was there that the majority of the casualties occurred. The firing line acted as a containing force and advanced slowly so as to give time to the Dorsets to develop what appeared to be a turning movement against the hostile left and to allow of effective artillery preparation. At about 12.20 p.m., as there was a considerable distance between the regiment's left and the right of the 18th Brigade, the local reserve was pushed in to fill the gap, with orders to utilize a small rise in the ground so as to get as near as possible to the Turkish trench before opening fire. From this portion it was intended to use covering fire to enable the three remaining double companies to advance. The firing line gradually gained ground on some 200 yards front while the Dorsets were swinging to the north. At about 1.30 the enemy left the trench in front in masses. They were then at some 700 yards and too distant to close with, so every available Maxim and rifle opened rapid fire and a message was sent back asking the guns to support. The guns had the target of a lifetime, as the Turks were retreating like one man and the ground was as flat as a table. They could not avail themselves of it, however, as there were only about one hundred rounds per gun with the whole of the force and they did not dare expend ammunition freely. As a result only comparatively few hostile dead and wounded were found in the trenches. The regiment pushed on, hoping to come to closer quarters with the Turks. On their arrival just north of the old fort, the enemy again opened fire from the edge of the woods. They were cleared out by rifle and Maxim fire.

The brigade then advanced to the Turkish camp, which was captured, and burned. A large quantity of medical stores, of which the force was very short, was found in the camp. In this action, Major Fordham, Captains Saxton and McCleverty were severely wounded, and Major St. John and Lieutenant Burn Murdoch slightly wounded. Of the Indian ranks six were killed and Subadar Ganda and fifty-one I.O.R.s were wounded. The report of the O.C. 20th Punjabis has the following note : " Throughout the day all officers did well, the difficulty being to restrain them, but I am especially grateful to my D.C.C.s Major Fordham, Major St. John, Captain Finnis and Captain McCleverty for the gallantry with which they led their men."

The next day was spent in collecting the wounded and putting them on board transports. The Turks withdrew towards Basra.

During the night of Thursday, 19th November, while the regiment was on outpost duty, six Kambar Khel Afridis deserted with their rifles and equipment. This was a great misfortune to the regiment ; but the previously expressed reluctance on the part of all Mohammedans against fighting in Iraq and the well-known intensity of the religious prejudices of the Afridis in particular explained the occurrence while not mitigating its seriousness. In this connection it was later ascertained from the Turks that the deserters refused to fight against the British, and gave as their reason for desertion the desire to get up to Baghdad to do reverence to their saint's tomb. In consequence of the above circumstance, Sir Arthur Barrett cabled to India strongly recommending that the regiment be sent to France at once. The regiment was immediately embarked on H. T. *Ekma*, and after remaining on board for four days was transferred to the *Mejedieh*, a river steamer, and taken to Basra, which had already been captured by the 6th Division. General Delamain, the Brigade Commander, deplored the loss of what he had considered one of his finest units, and shortly after arrival in Basra a reply was received to Sir Arthur

Barrett's cable to the effect that too much notice had been taken of the desertion of six men, and as the 20th Infantry had done well and had a great reputation they were to remain with the force.

On arrival in Basra the regiment with the rest of the brigade were accommodated in the Kesla Barracks—the old Turkish barracks and very dirty. On Friday, 4th December, Lieutenant-Colonel Rattray with A, B, G, and H Companies and 1/2nd Squadron 33rd Cavalry, moved out to Shaiba to protect Basra's left flank and to watch for any advance from Nasriyeh. He was relieved by Major St. John on the 15th, and on 5th January the wing was relieved by the 104th Rifles and returned to Basra. The next day the regiment took over the policing of Basra city from the 117th Mahrattas.

The situation in the city at this time was bad. Sniping was almost continuous and raids by Arabs from the surrounding villages were nightly occurrences. As soon as the regiment took over the city, they commenced an active programme of offensive action. Headquarters were located in the Serai, with posts at every gate of the city and constant patrols by day and night. This, however, had been proved insufficient, so neighbouring areas were searched for arms, ambushes were laid and villages in the district were rounded up and thoroughly searched. All these counter-raids were commenced before dawn, after seemingly casual reconnaissances, and their effect was immediately and completely successful. For the first time since its occupation by the British, Basra was quiet and peaceful, and both the troops and the local inhabitants could carry on their work without danger from raiders or snipers.

1915

January passed peacefully, but the Turks from Nasriyeh were gradually moving closer to Shaiba. On 8th February the annual floods came down and inundated the country between Basra and Shaiba, making communications very difficult. For 6 miles the water stood up to the knees of troops. On 18th February the 16th Brigade marched across the floods to Shaiba. The battalion was detached for rearguard with orders to march to Shwebda, a place some 6 miles to the south-west of Shaiba, and some 17 miles from Basra. The two supply columns were greatly delayed, and as there was also a severe shumal blowing, the main body marched away and left the rearguard to shepherd the transport. The convoy marched at 12.20 p.m. to Zobeir. There they were fired on by mounted Arabs, who were quickly dispersed by machine-gun fire. They were a portion of a force under Sheikh Ajaimi, which was situated close to Shaiba. The Sheikh of Zobeir asked the O.C. not to proceed to Shwebda, as he considered it unsafe. However, he was finally forced to accompany the convoy and the advance was continued. It was pitch-dark and raining heavily. Finding Shwebda was a pretty difficult proposition, and it was only by the blind wells that the place was located, at about 10 p.m. There was no trace of the main column. A perimeter camp was aligned by the aid of electric torches, and with great difficulty the convoy was got inside. It was still raining steadily. The situation was very unsafe, as the rearguard was only 12 miles from Naikaila, Ajaimi's headquarters, with no information as to the whereabouts of the main body. At 7 a.m., however, after an anxious night, they were relieved to see the 16th Brigade and a detachment of cavalry arrive at Shwebda from Shaiba. Owing to movements of the enemy cavalry the main body had been forced to go to Shaiba for the night, and the company, which had been sent to inform the rearguard of the change, had missed the convoy at Zobeir.

The 16th Infantry Brigade halted at Shwebda on 20th February and sent back all spare transport to Shaiba. The

G.O.C. then heard that Ajaimi's force, which was situated only 8 miles distant to the west, was being augmented by large reinforcements. It was considered unwise to risk an attack, and on the 21st the British force at Shwebda withdrew, quite unmolested, to Shaiba. On the 22nd the battalion returned to Basra, and on the 23rd moved out to camp at Makina Masus. The next day they made another march, rapid in spite of the floods, to Shaiba. On the 25th a considerable force of the enemy's cavalry, magnified by the mirage, approached close to Shaiba ; but, on coming within range of the Mountain Battery, were forced to withdraw after a short skirmish with cavalry. Shaiba entrenchment was commenced in the afternoon.

During the night of 26th/27th February, while the battalion was on outpost duty at Shaiba, Havildar Mir Akbar, an Afridi—a most capable N.C.O.—deserted with his rifle and his kit. (The whole Afridi piquet might have gone with him had it not been for the Lance Naik (an Afridi) and the signaller (a Khattack), who threatened to shoot anyone who joined Mir Akbar.) As a result the regiment was returned to Makina Masus. There was intense feeling throughout the ranks against the Afridi company, and the other Mohammedans as well as Sikhs and Dogras complained openly that they had again been robbed of their opportunity for service. On Monday, 1st March, the Sikh and Dogra I.O.s petitioned the C.O. for permission to return to Shaiba as a six-company battalion, leaving the transfrontier Pathans behind. On Wednesday, Sir Arthur Barrett saw the B.O.s and I.O.s, and told them that he knew the regiment was essentially loyal and that he was very sorry for their position. His recommendations to A.H.Q. that the 20th Infantry be given a chance in another area had not been acted upon. When on 2nd April he handed over command to Sir John Nixon, he said with reference to the occurrence : " In my opinion there must

To illustrate fighting near Shaiba.

Contours and Form lines only approximate
Heights in Feet
Scale

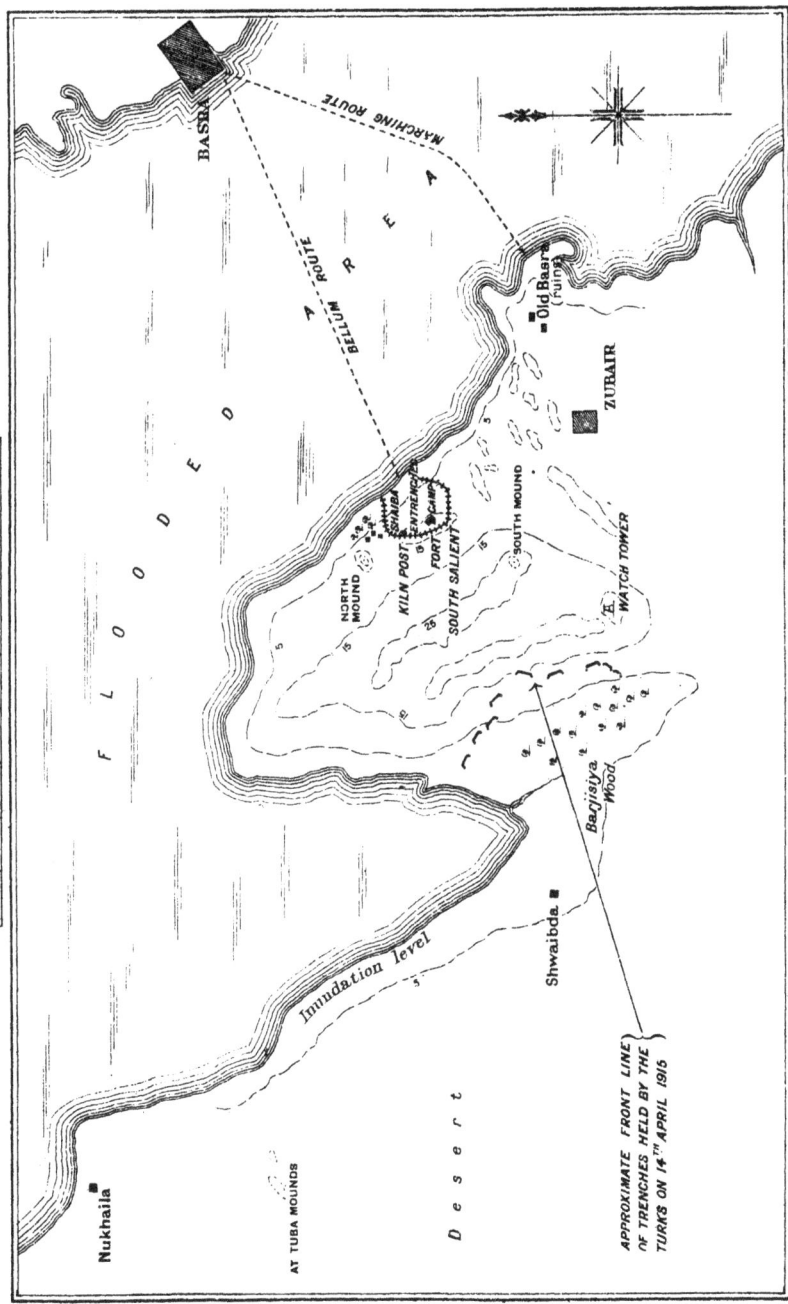

MILES 5   4   3   2   1   0   5 MILES

BASRA

MARCHING ROUTE

BELLUM ROUTE

F   L   O   O   D   E   D   A   R   E   A

Old Basra
(Pumps)

ZUBAIR

NORTH MOUND

KILN POST   SHAIBA
FORT   TRENCH

SOUTH SALIENT

SOUTH MOUND

WATCH TOWER

Barjisiya
Wood

Inundation level

Nukhaila

AT TUBA MOUNDS

D   e   s   e   r   t

Shwaibda

APPROXIMATE FRONT LINE
OF TRENCHES HELD BY THE
TURKS ON 14TH APRIL 1915

always be considerable risk in employing trans-frontier Pathans against Arabs. It is a pity that the reputation of a remarkably fine battalion should suffer because these men are serving in a country where their religious convictions clash with their sense of duty as soldiers."

On 12th April, during the attack by the Turks at Shaiba, the battalion, under Captains McCleverty and Churchill, worked hard in taking the 24th Punjabis to Shaiba across the floods in bellums—each bellum carrying eight men with their kit. The Arab boatmen refused to go, so the Regiment had to pole the bellums across the flood. On that night there were further desertions among the Bajauris and Buneris.

During the early hours of the 13th, the party under Captain McCleverty had a narrow escape. They had reached Shaiba at 22 hours, with the 24th Punjabis, and found the place being sniped and star-shelled by the enemy. They left again at midnight and at 04.30 hours Captain McCleverty found that his rear party had become separated from Captain Churchill and was constantly getting stuck on the mud. Suddenly, quite close, he saw a bellum containing Arabs. They challenged and he opened fire. The Arabs drew back and some Turks advanced through the water to his east, while two bellums approached on the west. His party killed several of the Turks and apparently hit some Arabs too. As it became light a swarm of bellums and men on foot pursued the party. His bellums stuck and he had to leave them and retire through the water. His party was almost surrounded when he came across a bellum full of the 24th Punjabis. They opened fire to support Captain McCleverty and the Turks at once retreated, evidently suspecting an ambush. The 20th Infantry lost twenty-two men, but accounted for many Turks and Arabs. It was a fortunate escape from a dangerous position.

During May and June the regiment was engaged in

c

patrolling and controlling the city of Basra.   On 27th June
they embarked for Qala Salih, having been relieved by the
67th Punjabis.   The next two months were spent there in
police work.   On 28th July, Major R. S. St. John took over
command from Captain B. H. Finnis, Lieutenant-Colonel
Rattray having been sent on the 16th to the 12th Division
as D.A.Q.M.G.   On Thursday, 26th August, the regiment
was relieved by the 2/7th Gurkha Rifles and embarked for
Amara on board the *Mejedieh*.   At Amara they were transferred to the P.2 and two barges and proceeded to Ali-al-
Gharbi, where they arrived on Saturday, 28th August,
rejoining the 16th Brigade, which was under the command
of Brigadier-General Delamain.

On Sunday, 12th September, the whole force from Ali
Gharbi advanced 12 miles to Omaiyeh.   The 20th Infantry,
under Major St. John, formed a part of the advance guard.
The weather was very severe—terrific heat and no wind.
Many heat casualties resulted among the British troops.
The advance was continued the following day, and on the
14th at 07.00 hours the force reached Shaikh Sa'ad, which
had been evacuated by the Turks on the 12th.   On Saturday, 18th September, the 20th Infantry formed a part of a
force which moved forward at 17.00 hours to induce the
Turks to show their positions.   The force was commanded
by Major Carnegy of the 7th Hariana Lancers, and consisted
of one squadron 7th Hariana Lancers, one section 76th
Battery R.F.A., and the 20th Infantry.   They bivouacked
on the river bank 5 miles from the Turkish position.
When the moon went down the enemy opened a heavy
fusillade with star-shells and rifle-fire—also coloured flares
all along his lines.   At dawn the force advanced to within
3 miles of the Turks.   Our cavalry got within 500 yards
of the enemy, but they, except for firing at the cavalry,
remained inactive.   That evening the British force returned
to Shaikh Sa'ad.   They found the division all ready to

advance, as some flocks of sheep had been given by the mirage the appearance of a large body of troops in pursuit of Major Carnegy's force.

While at Shaikh Sa'ad the division was greatly troubled by snipers, who were finally silenced by successful ambushes laid by the battalion.

On Sunday, 24th September, the 20th Infantry formed the vanguard of the advance guard of Column A of the 6th Division. An advance was to be made to the Chahela sand-hills, which were within distant artillery range of the Turkish position at Ess Sinn. The hills were occupied by 7.30 hours and the enemy's position kept under observation. There was very little movement to be seen. At 11.00 hours the regiment was relieved by the 2/7th Gurkhas and went into bivouac. The bivouac was shelled from time to time, but little damage resulted. On Monday, 27th September, the 12th Brigade on the left bank consolidated its position facing the Turks.

At 17.30 hours on 27th September the 16th Brigade advanced towards the enemy's lines at Ess Sinn, on the right bank of the river, and, after proceeding a short distance, started to entrench. Their orders were to make as much dust and display as possible, so as to deceive the Turks and make them think that the main attack would be carried out along both banks of the river. In this they were successful, though they failed to draw the enemy's fire.

At 19.00 hours the withdrawal commenced, and the 20th Infantry led the 16th Brigade across the bridge of boats to the left bank of the river to " Clery's " Post, which had been established at the south-east corner of the Suwada Marsh. Here the 20th Infantry and the 104th Rifles were attached to the 17th Infantry Brigade under Brigadier-General Hoghton.

The Battle of Kut-el-Amara

At 02.00 hours on 28th September the force left Clery's Post to make a night march to the position of deployment, a point about 5,000 yards east of the northern section of the hostile position and marked by its position in relation to the south-west corner of the Suwaikieh Marsh.

The march was guided by an officer of the Royal Engineers, who had obtained a compass bearing in a personal reconnaissance but had been unable to make a thorough reconnaissance owing to the activity of hostile horsemen and fear of arousing the enemy's suspicions.

An operation map prepared as a result of air reconnaissance had been issued to all units. This gave a very good indication of the relative positions of the different topographical features, but the wide variation of its magnetic bearings with those obtained by the Engineer officer made it inadvisable to include any compass bearing in the orders issued to the column. At that time the Air Force in Mesopotamia had not got a really reliable compass for aeroplane work.

General Hoghton's force led the column, preceded by a small advance guard, formed by C Company of the 20th Infantry, the six battalions moved in column of route—two battalions abreast at close interval—with small flank guards and the transport on the right flank.

At 04.45 hours the advanced guard reported marsh on three sides and the column halted and deployed for attack.

It was later found that the Suwaikieh Marsh had been struck at a point a little to the north of that intended; consequently, when the advance commenced, on the bearings laid down in orders, General Hoghton's force came up against the Ataba Marsh. Thinking it was a small isolated marsh not marked on the map, the advance was continued, leaving the marsh on the left.

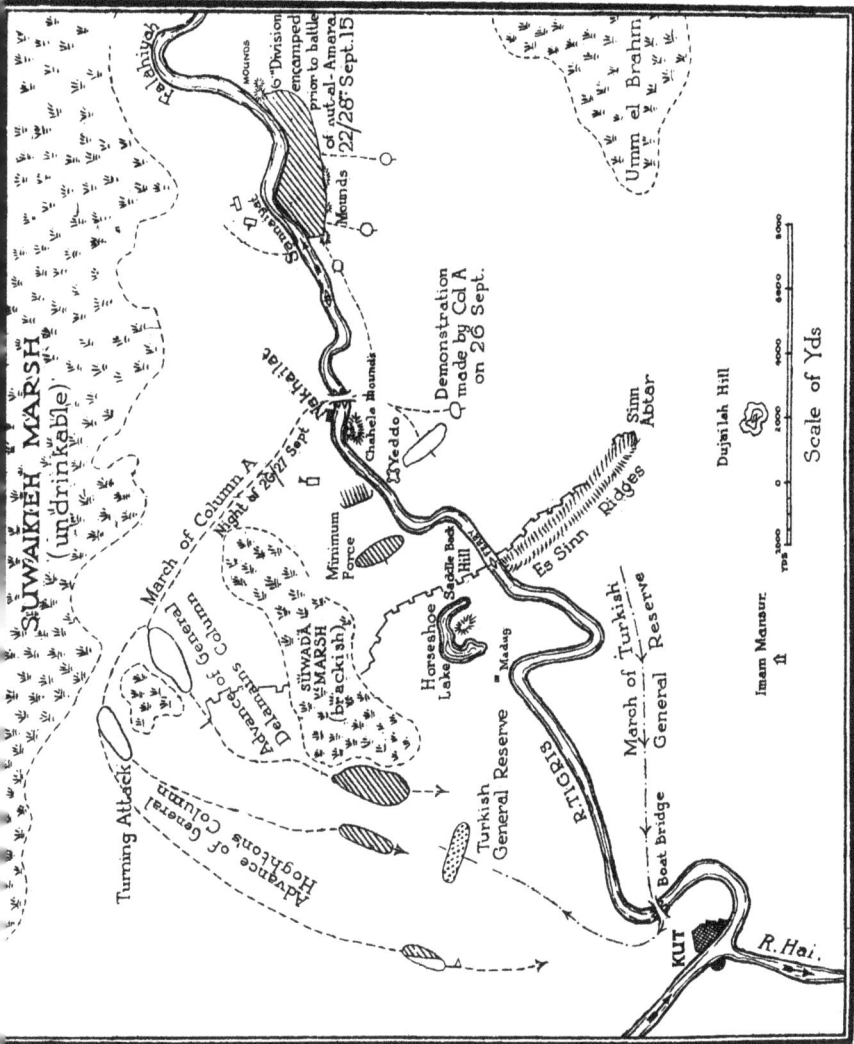

Plan of the Battle of Kut-al-Amara

When it got light, about 06.00 hours, and it was discovered that it was the Ataba Marsh, it was decided to carry on rather than go back and start afresh.

This was really a fortunate error, as by proceeding round the Ataba Marsh the enemy's position was completely turned. For the advance from the position of deployment General Hoghton deployed his infantry in two lines on a 1,200 yards front ; the leading line consisting, from the right, of the Brigade Machine Guns, the 20th Infantry, Oxford Light Infantry and 22nd Punjabis, and the second line of the 104th Rifles, 103rd Mahrattas and 119th Infantry.

The artillery were on the left rear and the cavalry forward on the right, so as to be able to move round and discover the enemy's rear positions. As far as the 20th Infantry was concerned nothing of moment happened until 10.00 hours, when a strong hostile force was seen advancing from the south-south-west, apparently directed against the right flank of General Hoghton's force.

The 20th were ordered to attack this force.

The battalion was launched in three successive lines straight at the enemy. Under heavy rifle and artillery fire they pushed on without halting, and when about 400 yards from the enemy they fixed bayonets and charged. The Turks refused the collision and withdrew rapidly. The Turkish artillery tried in vain to check the advance, but they had inflicted severe casualties before they were silenced by the 76th Battery R.F.A.

This advance drove back the Turks for 2 miles, and its rapidity saved the battalion many casualties.

The heat was severe, and there was a burning, dusty wind, and the question of water for the troops was becoming acute ; the marshes through which the advance had been made were all salty.

Owing to lack of sufficient telephone wire, communication between General Hoghton and General Delamain was interrupted between 13.00 hours and 14.15 hours. By 14.30 hours the 16th and 17th Brigades had joined forces and were resting in a hollow west of the Suwada Marsh. Here the 20th Infantry and 104th Rifles again came under the orders of the 16th Infantry Brigade.

At 16.50 hours General Delamain's force began a further advance round the south-western corner of the Suwada Marsh, with the intention of assisting the attack of the 18th Brigade by taking in reverse the Turkish position between the Suwada and Horseshoe Marshes.

The 17th Brigade led with the 16th Brigade in echelon on the right rear.

At 17.30 hours strong hostile reinforcements were seen moving from the southwards towards the Horseshoe Marsh.

General Delamain immediately issued orders for the whole force to change front to the right and attack these reinforcements, the 16th Brigade being echeloned back to the right of the 17th Brigade.

The Turks at once took up a defensive position in a dry canal and opened a heavy rifle-fire, supported by four field guns, which latter were quickly silenced by our artillery.

Major St. John formed the 20th into two lines and fixing bayonets launched them straight at the Turks, whose position was about a mile and a half distant.

In spite of heat and thirst the men went forward with great dash—without halting or firing a shot they went straight for the Turks with the bayonet. The Turks could not face it and their retreat rapidly became a rout.

By 18.45 hours the battalion had captured four Krupp field-guns, two machine-guns, a large amount of rifle and gun ammunition, some prisoners and the enemy's main position.

The fact that the battalion suffered less casualties than other battalions was largely due to the rapidity with which the attack was carried out.

The officer commanding the Dorsets told Major St. John that the advance of the 20th was one of the finest things he had ever seen—high praise from a man commanding a battalion like the Dorsets.

As soon as the dry canal had been captured the G.O.C. stopped the advance and the troops settled down in the canal for the night.

The casualties this day were :—

Captain B. H. Finnis	Wounded	
,, P. H. McCleverty	,,	
Subadar Kapura	,,	
,, Masin Khan	,,	
Jemadar Hazrat Shah	,,	
,, Kashmir Singh	,,	
,, Aslam	,,	

I.O.R.s Wounded, 120 ; Killed, 15 ; Missing, 9.

The battalion had gone into action with a strength of five hundred and thirty.

The regiment was later heartily congratulated by General Delamain, Sir John Nixon and General Townshend on their splendid work throughout the day.

Wednesday, 29th September. During the night the retreat of the Turks became a rout, and even the posts facing the 18th Brigade were evacuated. At dawn a move was made to the river, where all the enemy's camps were found empty of men, but with stores and ammunition lying about everywhere. The Cavalry Brigade galloped forward and occupied Kut. The retreating Turks were located by aeroplanes, some 15 miles up the river. At noon the 16th Brigade made for Kut, where it arrived at 15.00 hours and bivouacked. During the night after the battle mounted Arabs had ridden on to the battlefield and by moonlight stripped and looted both British and Turkish wounded, some of whom it had been impossible to find until daybreak.

On 6th October and the three days following the regiment
marched with the rest of the 16th Brigade to Azizieh, some
50 miles up the river, where they encamped. The next
fortnight was spent in brigade fatigues and outpost duty.
On Saturday, 23rd October, two Adam Khel Afridis deserted
from a piquet, killed one sepoy and seriously wounded a
havildar—both Sikhs. Again the Afridis had proved
themselves utterly untrustworthy, and again the regiment
was ordered back to the base. Of course the Sikhs and
the Dogras felt very bitter. General Delamain was sym-
pathetic, and fully endorsed Major St. John's recommendations that the Afridis be at once disbanded and their
places taken by Khuttacks and Dogras. Every one
realized that it was very hard on the remainder of the
battalion, as well as a great waste of splendid fighting
troops to employ them at the base ; but there was no help
for it, and on the 27th October the battalion embarked
on S.S. *Blosse-Lynch*, and proceeded down the river. At
Kut, which was reached on the 29th, General Melliss asked
Sir John Nixon if he might have five companies of the
20th to strengthen his brigade. He did not dare take the
whole regiment, as he said he was already doubtful of
such Afridis as he had. The battalion continued on its
way, and on 1st November arrived at Amara, where it
joined the 33rd Brigade under General Douglas. There
they remained until 16th July, 1916, mostly split up in
small detachments doing duty on the line of communication. One detachment remained at Qala Salih and another
at Filaifilah.

1916

In April the trans-frontier Pathans of the 20th Infantry
and those of all other units were collected in Basra, formed
into companies, fully equipped and sent off to German
East Africa, under the command of Captain Irwin of the

20th D.C.O. Infantry. There they acquitted themselves well, and did their best to remove the stain on their reputation. The battalion remained in Amara doing garrison duty there until the end of July.

The Move from Amara to join the 7th Division, July 16–July 19

At the end of July, 1916, orders were received that the battalion was to join the 21st Brigade, 7th Division, who were holding the Sannaiyat position. No. 2 Company, under Major McCleverty, with Second-Lieutenant Fitzgibbon, left Amara by river steamer on 30th July, 1916, in advance of the remainder of the battalion. They were held up at Ali Garbi for the 31st owing to rumours of a hostile Arab force on the right bank between that place and Sheikh Sa'ad. The company reached Sheikh Sa'ad on 1st August, and, leaving there on the 4th, in two parties, arrived at Arab Village early on the 5th. On 6th August the company marched to the Central Area of the Sannaiyat position and the following day to the reserve trenches. From there they took over the piquets on the right of the position, remaining there until the 12th and then returned to the Central Area. Another tour in the trenches (the company being attached to the 9th Bhopals) was commenced on 3rd September, during which the company held positions in the second line and later in the front line. The tour lasted ten days, and three of the Dogras were wounded— one being Sepoy Haku (6 feet 4 inches), who could not keep his head below the parapet.

In the meantime the detachment from Ezra's Tomb had rejoined the battalion at Amara on 28th August, having marched on 25th August. Prior to the move of the remainder of the battalion to join the 7th Division, Captain Hawes and Lieutenant Burn-Murdoch were transferred to the Depôt in India and Captain Churchill proceeded on

one month's leave. Captain Morton-Marshall, 130th Baluchis, was attached to the battalion and Lieutenants Kidd
and Fleming joined the battalion from the Depôt in India.
Lieutenant Kidd took over the duties of adjutant.

On 7th September the battalion (less No. 2 Company)
left Amara to join the 7th Division. Headquarters and
No. 1 Company went by steamer, arriving at Arab Village
on 9th September and No. 3 Company marched by half-
companies. E Company left Amara on the 6th under
Lieutenant Fleming, and F Company the following day
under Lieutenant Hayes. Captain Morton-Marshall, who
commanded the company, was admitted to hospital on
6th September.

No. 2 Company, on relief in the trenches on 14th September, joined the battalion at Arab Village, and when
on 17th September No. 3 Company arrived, the battalion,
which had only three companies, was complete.

The other units making up the 21st Brigade were 2nd
Black Watch, 9th Bhopals and 1/8th Gurkha Rifles.

Trench Warfare at Sannaiyat

The position at Sannaiyat, as held by the 7th Division
at the time, was organized in three areas, each occupied
by one brigade. Brigades moved in rotation about every
ten days. The Forward Area or trench system was divided
into four sections—right, centre, left and reserve—each
being held by one battalion. This system extended from
the Suwaikieh Marsh on the right to the River Tigris on
the left, the right being drawn back along the marsh.
The distance between the Turkish trenches and ours was
about 100 yards on the left of the system and increased
to about 1,000 yards on the right. The whole front was
about 1,000 yards. There were four lines of trenches, the
fourth being the Reserve.

On 3rd October the battalion moved to the Forward

Area and took over the left section. This first tour of the battalion was uneventful; but as it was the first time the battalion had experienced trench warfare, every one had a lot to learn. The fact that No. 2 Company had previously done a tour in the trenches proved of great value. The men quickly adapted themselves to the new conditions, and soon learnt not to look over the top unnecessarily. The Turks had a mortar firing 100-pound bombs. These burst with a terrific explosion, but fortunately did little damage beyond breaking some of the glasses in the mess dug-out. The casualties during this tour—five I.O.R.s killed and seven wounded—were mostly due to snipers.

On relief on 14th October the battalion moved to the Central Area and went into camp there. While here the M.G. Section, under Second-Lieutenant Hayes, which had been with the Brigade M.G. Company, rejoined the battalion, leaving their guns with the company, all Indians having been replaced by British personnel.

Lewis guns were issued to us here, and we had a busy time training officers and men in their use.

On 3rd November the battalion again moved to the Forward Area and took over the centre section. The next day while the front-line trenches had been temporarily evacuated (except for sentries), in order to admit of the artillery registering on the Turkish front line, four Yusufzais deserted and went over to the Turkish position. In consequence of this occurrence the Divisional Commander (General Fane) ordered all the Yusufzais in the battalion to be put under arrest and sent back to the Central Area to the battalion dump. Lieutenant-Colonel Fordham at once protested, and the matter was represented to General Cobbe, the Corps Commander. He agreed with Colonel Fordham that no useful purpose would be served by such action, and that unless it was intended to take the Yusafzais right away from the battalion they must be trusted.

Colonel Fordham's view was fully justified, as there were no more desertions.

On 13th November the battalion was relieved and moved to the Rearward Area. The tour was a peaceful one, except for the occasional shelling of the third line, in which were Battalion Headquarters, by Turkish 5·9-inch guns. This did little damage, but made office work unpopular. While in the Rearward Area, the new company of Kashmiri Mohammedans joined the battalion under Second-Lieutenant Burgess and were posted two platoons to No. 1 Company and two platoons to No. 4 Company. The Sikhs of the old A. and H. Corps, who had been joined in No. 1 Company on the departure of the Afridis, were again divided and H Company went to No. 4 Company. The companies were re-named A, B, C and D. At this time an order was received to reduce kit to a minimum and the prospect of an advance pleased every one.

On 3rd December the battalion again moved to the Forward Area, taking over the centre section. Two days later, however, they were relieved and occupied the reserve section. On 14th December the battalion, supported by artillery, made a demonstration on the right flank, the artillery having made a demonstration on the previous day. The Turks, however, did not treat this seriously, and only put over a few rounds of shrapnel which burst too high, wounding two men. Having drawn the enemy's gunfire, the battalion returned.

On relief on 17th December the battalion went into camp in the Central Area, where Christmas was spent. On 26th December Major Finnes was transferred to hospital, followed on 2nd January by Major McCleverty.

1917

On 5th January the battalion crossed to the right bank of the river, and on the following day took over the River

Piquet Line from the right, at Croftons O.P., to Chahela. This line had previously been held by units of 3rd Division. The battalion was relieved on 22nd January by 1/8th Gurkha Rifles and returned to camp on the left bank in the Rearward Area. On 27th January the battalion again marched to the right bank and took over the River Piquet Line with A and B Companies only, Headquarters with C and D Companies going into the Narrows Camp in Brigade Reserve. While in this camp the Corps Commander (General Cobbe) paid it a visit, during which the camp was unexpectedly shelled. Luckily the camp was well provided with shelter trenches, and more amusement than damage was caused. A number of shells fell in the camp, one of them hitting the doctor's tent. Lieutenant Agate, I.M.S., had, fortunately for him, already left it.

C and D Companies relieved A and B Companies on 2nd February, and the latter, with Headquarters, returned to the Rearward Area on the left bank.

The next day A and B Companies took over the right flank trenches on the extreme right of the Forward Area, while Headquarters marched to the Central Area, where they were joined the next day by C and D Companies, who had been relieved in the River Piquet Line. On 11th February the battalion (less two companies) moved to the reserve section of the Forward Area, where they were joined by A and B Companies. After two days, however, the battalion moved on relief to the Central Area.

Attack on the Sannaiyat Position, 17th February, 1917

While in this area orders were received that the battalion would take part in an attack on the Turkish position at Sannaiyat, and the attack was practised on a model which had been dug from aeroplane photos. The battalion practised the attack in four lines—A and B Company first and second line, C and D Companies third and fourth line. A and D Companies were on the right and companies were on a two-platoon front. The front on which the battalion was to attack was about 150 yards, the objective being the enemy second line. The 1/8th Gurkha Rifles were to attack on the left of the battalion, but the right flank was in the air.

The attack was rehearsed for three days, and on the evening of 16th February the battalion marched to the reserve trenches. During the night it rained heavily, and the trenches became so muddy that it was difficult to get along them. Zero hour was originally fixed for 12.00 hours, but, owing to the delay caused by the mud, it was found necessary to postpone the attack until 14.00 hours.

The battalion went over, preceded by a heavy barrage, and captured their objective. Of the British officers, Captain Churchill and Lieutenant Fitzgibbon with the first and second line got over safely, but the former was killed soon after the objective had been reached. Second-Lieutenant Burgess, who went over with the third line, was killed when half-way to the Turkish trenches, and S.M. Masin Khan, who was with the fourth line, was killed while leaving our trenches. All went well until about 16.30 hours, when the Turks delivered a strong counter-attack on our right flank and centre, supported by a heavy barrage. The battalion was forced back, and, as there was by then only a very small party of the battalion in reserve, it was decided not to renew the attack. Eighteen Turkish prisoners were captured and brought back when the battalion withdrew. It was unfortunate that there was no British officer left alive to organize the defence on the right flank, which formed a difficult salient.

At about 18.00 hours the battalion was withdrawn to

SUBADAR MAJOR MASIN KHAN
Killed in Action at Sannaiyat on the 17th February 1917

the reserve section to reorganize, and the following day marched to the Central Area.

The casualties on 17th February, in addition to those previously mentioned, were Jemadar Jhanda Singh and sixty-seven I.O.R.s killed, five I.O.s and one hundred and sixty-nine I.O.R.s wounded, one I.O. and eighteen I.O.R.s missing—a total of two B.O.s, 8 I.O.s and two hundred and fifty-four I.O.R.s.

On 22nd February another attack was made on the Turkish position and the battalion moved up to the reserve trenches. At about 16.00 hours on 23rd February news was received that the Turks were evacuating their Sannaiyat position, and on 24th February the battalion advanced in support to the 2nd Black Watch as far as the Suwada position, which was occupied without opposition. The following day the battalion marched as far as a point about 4 miles north of Kut, but on 26th February was temporarily attached to Line of Communication Defences and established posts back to the Suwada position, Headquarters with A and D Companies at the latter place, C Company at the former, with B Company at the north end of the Megasis bend of the river, about half-way between.

The battalion remained as above until relieved by the 14th Sikhs on 6th March. Large bodies of mounted Arabs were seen in the distance from Suwada, but they did not come near the camp. Otherwise life was peaceful after the exertions of the past few weeks.

Between 17th February and 6th March Second-Lieutenants Fleming, Berkeley, and Hodgkins and drafts to the total of one hundred and twenty I.O.R.s had joined the battalion. The former had been Brigade Transport officer since the battalion joined the 21st Brigade in September, 1916, and for his work in this capacity he was mentioned in despatches. The following awards were given to the battalion as a result of these operations : Lance Naick Churu I.O.M., Sepoy Bachitar I.D.S.M., both Dogras of B Company.

The March to Baghdad

On 7th March the battalion marched to Shumran and took over a piquet line across the loop of the river from the 93rd Infantry. They remained there until relieved by the 2nd Rajputs on 12th March, when they marched to Imam Mahdi. The following day a distance of 16 miles was covered to Ash, and on 14th March 20 miles to Aziziyah. On 15th March Zeur was reached, a distance of 14 miles, and on 16th and 17th March Bustan and Dialah, distances of 14 and 15 miles respectively. When within 2 miles of the latter place, orders were received to send back two companies to relieve the Dorsets at Bawi. C and D Companies under Captain Morton-Marshall, were sent, and did not rejoin the battalion until 23rd March.

A halt having been made at Dialah for one day, on 19th March the battalion, less two companies, marched to Baghdad and again came under the orders of 7th Division. On 21st March the 21st Brigade was rejoined at Hassaiwa, about 14 miles up-stream.

During the march from Suwada the battalion moved independently and consequently the march was comfortable, except for the dust which in places could not be avoided. After four months of trench warfare at Sannaiyat the battalion had quickly regained its marching prowess, and on arrival at Baghdad all ranks were very fit.

On 22nd March the 21st Brigade commenced to close back on Baghdad, and on 25th March went into camp about 2 miles north-west of that place. B Company, under Second-Lieutenant Fitzgibbon, marched to Nukhta on 26th March, a distance of about 20 miles towards Faluja, remaining there just over a week. The same day Lieutenant-Colonel Fordham was transferred to hospital, and the

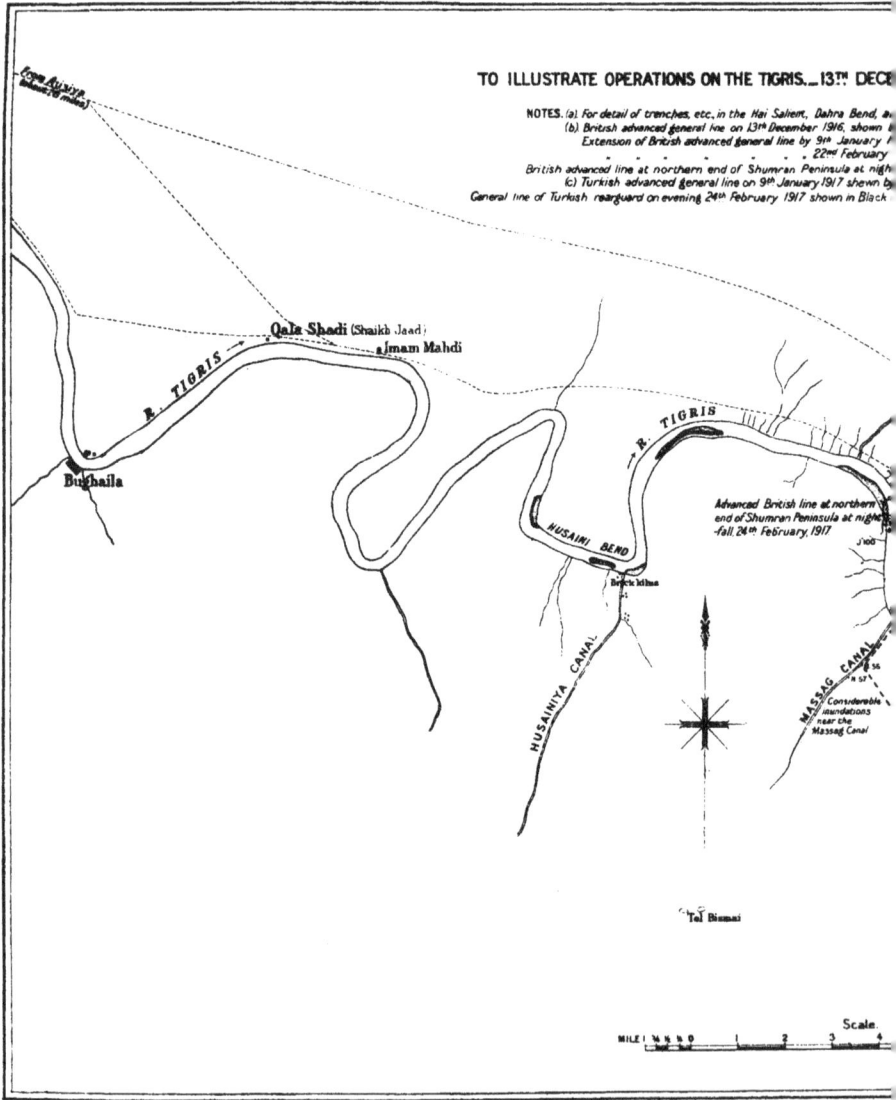

TO ILLUSTRATE OPERATIONS ON THE TIGRIS.—13TH DECE

NOTES. (a) For detail of trenches, etc, in the Hai Salient, Dahra Bend, a
(b) British advanced general line on 13th December 1916, shown
Extension of British advanced general line by 9th January 1
_ _ _ _ _ _ _ _ _ _ _ . 22nd February
British advanced line at northern end of Shumran Peninsula at nigh
(c) Turkish advanced general line on 9th January 1917 shewn by
General line of Turkish rearguard on evening 24th February 1917 shown in Black

From Azizia
(about 18 miles)

R. TIGRIS

Qala Shadi (Shaikh Jaad)
Imam Mahdi

Bughaila

R. TIGRIS

HUSAINI BEND

Advanced British line at northern
end of Shumran Peninsula at night-
fall. 24th February, 1917

Brick Kilns

HUSAINIYA CANAL

MASSAG CANAL

Considerable
inundations
near the
Massag Canal

Tel Bismai

MILE ½ ¼ ¼ 0   1   2   3   4
                              Scale.

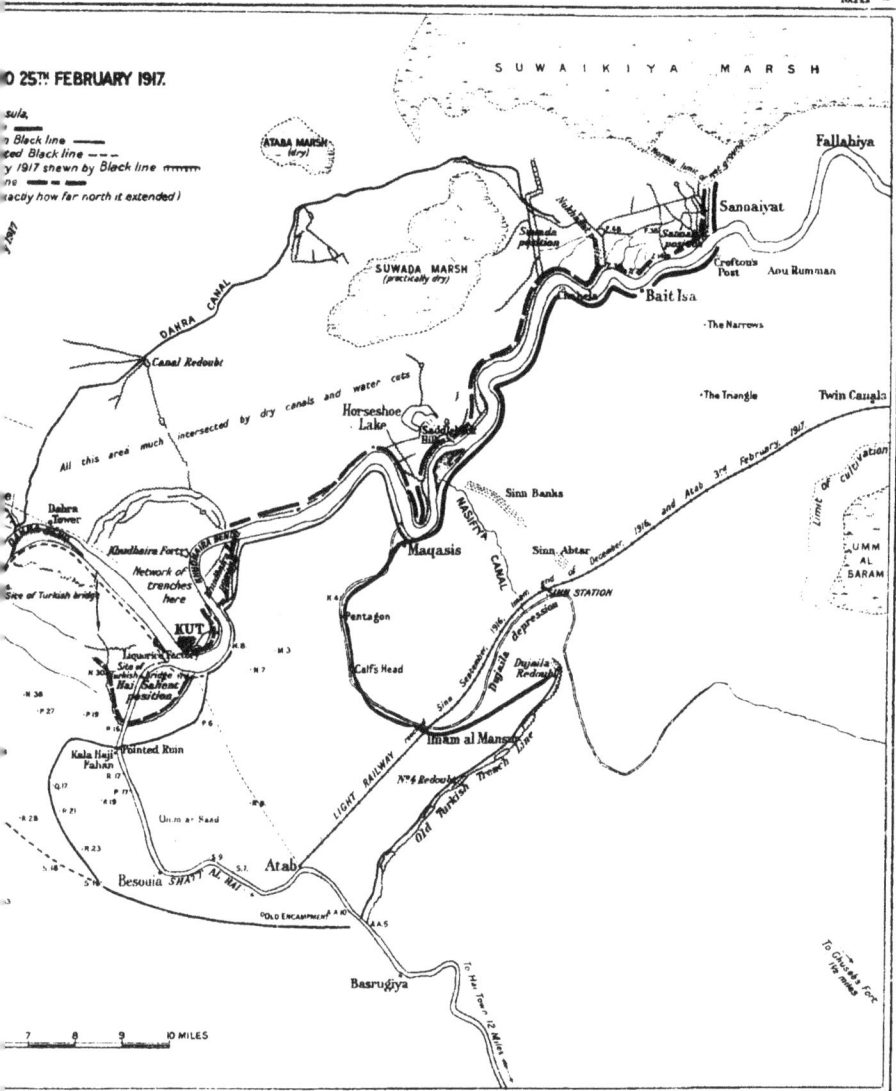

MAP 4

O 25TH FEBRUARY 1917.

sula.
n Black line ——
ted Black line — — —
y 1917 shewn by Black line ⚏⚏⚏
ne
aculy how far north it extended)

SUWAIKIYA MARSH

Fallahiya

ATABA MARSH
(dry)

Sannaiyat

Crefton's Post

Abu Rumman

SUWADA MARSH
(practically dry)

Suwada position

Sannaiyat position

DAHRA CANAL

Bait Isa

Canal Redoubt

The Narrows

All this area much intersected by dry canals and water cuts

Horseshoe Lake

Saddle Hill

The Triangle

Twin Canals

Sinn Banks

HASIFIYA CANAL

end of December 1916, and Atab 3rd February, 1917

Limit of cultivation

UMM AL SARAM

Dahra Tower

Maqasis

Sinn Abtar

2nd of December 1916

Khadhaira Fortn

Network of trenches here

Site of Turkish bridge

KUT

Sinn Station

SINN STATION

Pentagon

Liquorice Factn

Site of Turkish Bridge

Hai Salient positions

Calfs Head

Sinn Seesaw, 1916

Dujaila depression

Dujaila Redoubt

Kala Haji Fahan

Pointed Ruin

Umm-a-Saad

Imam al Mansur

Nº4 Redoubt

Old Turkish Trench Line

LIGHT RAILWAY

Ataba

Besouia SHATT AL HAI

OLD ENCAMPMENT

To Chasaka Fort
½ miles

Basrugiya

To Hai Town 12 Miles

7   8   9   10 MILES

command of the battalion devolved on Captain Morton-Marshall.

Until 6th April the battalion occupied various portions of the Railway Piquet Line until relieved on that date by the 1st Gurkhas.

During this period Second-Lieutenant Raschen and a draft of one I.O. and twenty-four I.O.R.s joined the battalion, and Second-Lieutenant Berkeley was transferred to hospital.

The Advance to Samarra

On 6th April the battalion marched with 21st Brigade to Babi, a distance of 20 miles. The march was made by night, there being a good moon. On the following day the brigade marched to Kermeah, and on 8th April to Sumaikcheh. Beled railway station was reached on 9th April and the battalion went on alone to Beled village, which was entered without incident, and camped at the north-west corner of the village, where it remained until 15th April. On that day the battalion took over the right section of the outpost line north of Harbe from 28th Punjabis 19th Brigade, and the next day advanced at 14.00 hours and occupied a hill north-west of Al Khubn without casualties—the Turkish outposts withdrawing before our advance. On 17th April the battalion was relieved in the new outpost position by 2nd Black Watch and went back about a mile, where they camped for two days.

Battle of Istabulat

On 20th April orders were received to attack the Turks, who were holding a strong position astride the Dujail Canal, on the following day. The 21st Brigade were to attack on the right of the canal and the 19th on the left. Of the 21st Brigade the 9th Bhopals and 1/8th Gurkha

D

Rifles were in the first line, the Black Watch in support and the battalion in Brigade Reserve.

At 05.00 hours on 21st April the battalion moved to a preparatory position, and at about 07.30 hours A and C Companies under Second-Lieutenant Raschen and Captain Hayes went forward between the 1/8th Gurkha Rifles and the 9th Bhopals, the objective being a redoubt on the left centre of the enemy's position. On nearing the objective, A Company, who were leading, came under very heavy rifle and machine-gun fire and Second-Lieutenant Raschen was wounded. The companies established themselves on the high ground round the north-east corner of the old canal, whence they drove off two counter-attacks. At about 09.00 hours Headquarters and the remainder of the battalion moved forward to reinforce A and C Companies, whose casualties by this time numbered about twenty-five. Before this had been effected, however, orders were received to move forward in immediate support of the 2nd Black Watch, who were to press home an attack, supported by an artillery barrage, along the right bank of the Dujail Canal at 11.00 hours. Before starting, a message was received from the F.O.O. 20th Battery that the enemy was active on the right, and three platoons of B Company were therefore left in position on a ridge to watch the right flank. The remainder of the battalion moved across the open to the Dujail Canal and proceeded along the right bank until it came up with the Black Watch. This move was made under heavy shell-fire, but casualties were slight. In the meantime C Company, under Captain Hayes, had pushed forward and occupied an enemy trench connecting Redoubts A and B running north from the Western Redoubt. A bombing party and a platoon of B Company were sent forward to reinforce Captain Hayes after the arrival of the battalion at Black Watch Headquarters.

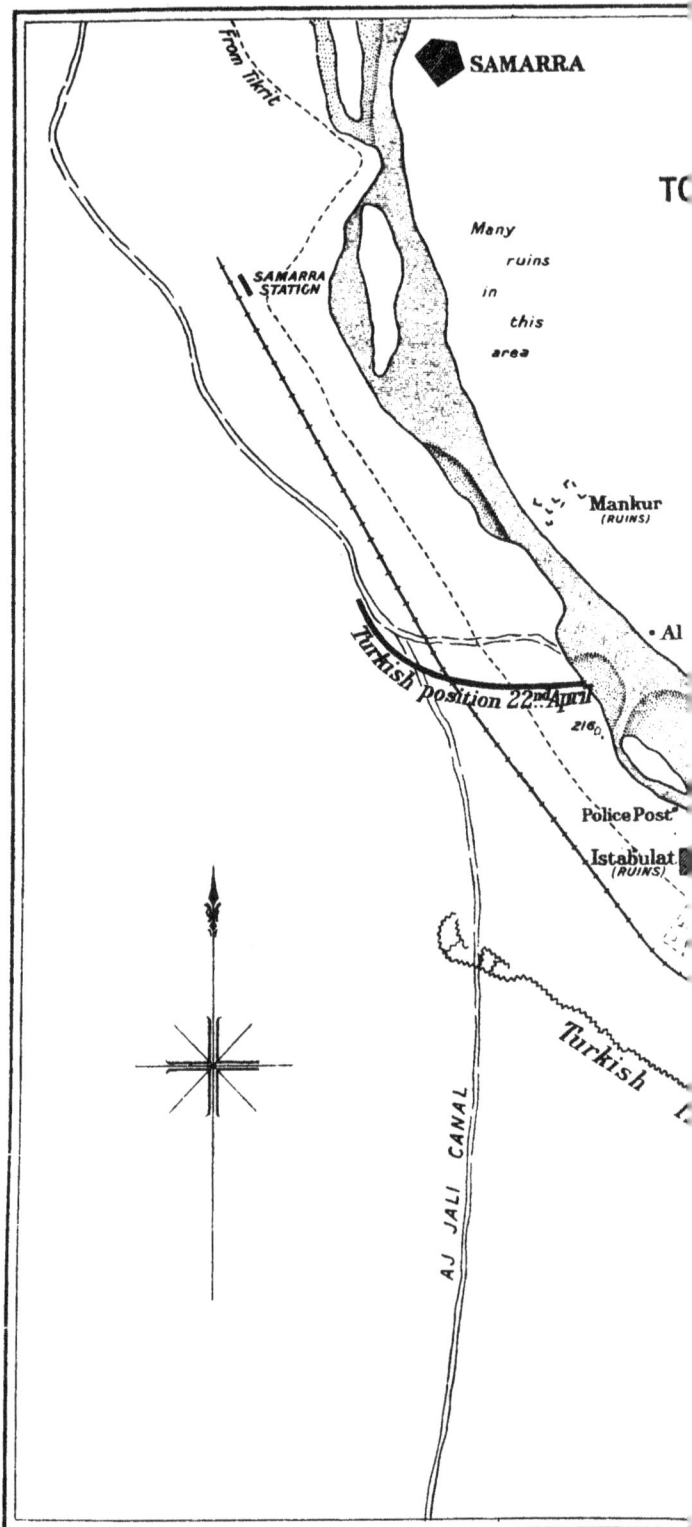

SAMARRA

TO

From Tikrit

SAMARRA
STATION

Many
ruins
in
this
area

Mankur
(RUINS)

· Al

Turkish Position 22nd April

216₀.

Police Post

Istabulat
(RUINS)

Turkish

AJ JALI CANAL

MAP 5

STRATE THE ACTION OF ISTABULAT.

21st and 22nd April, 1917.

SCALE OF MILES

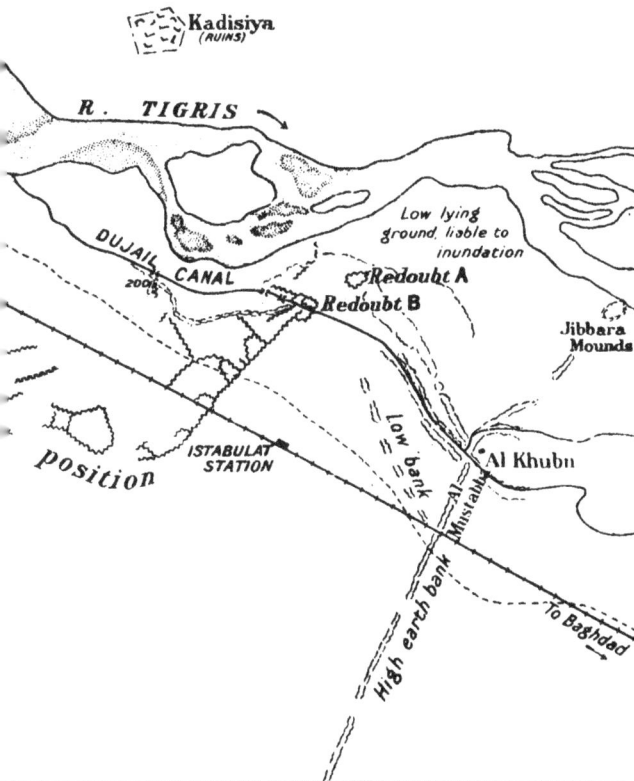

½ ¼ 0   1   2   3   4 MILES

Kadisiya
(RUINS)

R . TIGRIS

Low lying
ground, liable to
inundation

DUJAIL CANAL

200

Redoubt A

Redoubt B

Jibbara
Mounds

low bank

position

ISTABULAT
STATION

Al Khubn

Al Mustaha

High earth bank

To Baghdad

These positions were maintained throughout the day, no forward movement having been made owing to the barrage proving inefficient. At dusk B Company went forward to prolong Captain Hayes' right and fill the gap between his company and 9th Bhopals.

During the night the enemy retired with his usual skill, and although closely followed up, the 28th Brigade being in advance, he could not be made to stand again, and touch with him was eventually lost.

The battalion was again ordered to remain behind, this time to clean up the battlefield, while the rest of the brigade went on in pursuit. On 24th April the battalion marched to Samarra, where it rejoined the 21st Brigade.

The casualties in the battalion on 21st April were twelve I.O.R.s killed, and one B.O. and fifty-three I.O.R.s wounded. The following awards were given to men of the battalion for these operations : Captain Hayes an M.C., Hazara Singh a posthumous I.O.M.

The Hot Weather at Samarra

On 25th April Second-Lieutenant Berkeley rejoined the battalion and Major Morton-Marshall was transferred to hospital on 30th April, the command of the battalion devolving on Captain Kidd until Lieutenant-Colonel Fordham and Captain Hawes rejoined on 5th May.

On 9th May a draft of two I.O.s and two hundred and eighteen I.O.R.s joined the battalion, including two platoons of Kumaonis, mostly from the Burma Military Police. The Kumaonis were posted to D Company in place of the Sikhs of 15th and 16th Platoons, who, as the Sikhs had fallen so low in numbers, were transferred to the Sikh Platoons of A Company.

On 16th May Lieutenant Berkeley was again transferred to hospital, and on 25th May the battalion moved to a new camp about a mile up-stream of Samarra on the right bank. Here all ranks proceeded to make themselves comfortable, and preparations were made for the hot weather—tents dug down, etc. In due course the heavy kit, which had been dumped at Sannaiyat, arrived, and with the arrival of the canteen and frozen meat there was little to be desired. The day temperature was at times very high, the highest being 130° in an E.P. tent, but the nights were cool and every one kept very fit.

During June the following British officers joined the battalion : Captain Strover, 5th Light Infantry, Captain Bird, 29th Punjabis, and Lieutenant Hart, I.A.R.O. On arrival at Samarra the 9th Bhopals were replaced in the brigade by the 1st Guides.

During the hot weather the battalion took its turn in finding the garrison of the town of Samarra, which consisted of two platoons, and in digging a position on the left bank.

On 15th June Lieutenant Agate, I.M.S., was transferred to Basra for duty, his place being taken by Lieutenant Khan, I.M.S. On 19th June Lieutenant Hart was transferred to hospital and on 24th June Lieutenant O'Sullivan, 66th Punjabis, joined the battalion.

During June the following went on leave to India for one month : Colonel Fordham, Captain Bird, Lieutenants Barclay, Hayes and Fitzgibbon, ten I.O.s and about two hundred I.O.R.s.

On 12th September Captains Hawes and Strover left the battalion to take up the appointments of G.S.O. III, 17th Division, and G.S.O. III, 1st Corps, respectively, and on 9th October Captain H. R. D. Walker, 25th Punjabis, joined the battalion.

On 22nd October the Turks, who had remained at Tekrit during the hot weather, were reported to have advanced on both sides of the River Tigris to a point 5 miles up-stream of Samarra, and the division stood to arms. On the following day the 19th and 28th Brigades moved out to drive them back, the 21st Brigade taking over the Samarra defences on both banks. The battalion occupied the right and centre sections of the Al Ajik position on the right bank. On the 24th the division returned to its normal area, the Turks having withdrawn to Daur.

On 31st October Captain B. A. S. Brunskill, 79th Carnatic Infantry, joined the battalion.

The Advance to Tekrit

On 1st November the advance to Tekrit was commenced, the 21st Brigade being the only brigade to advance up the left bank. The remainder of the 1st Corps moved up the right bank.

The battalion left camp at Samarra at 22.15 hours, and, crossing to the left bank, advanced in reserve to the brigade to the Turkish (left bank) position at Daur. A small patrol of cavalry only was found in the position and they retired immediately. The brigade halted and, putting out outposts, to which the battalion was in reserve, remained there for the night.

On 3rd November the brigade advanced to a point just south of the Dauri Rocks, where they remained for the day, returning in the evening to their previous position. During the day the battle, which was proceeding on the right bank, was heard, and in the evening news was received that the Turks had been driven from their Daur position on that bank. At 22.30 hours on 4th November the battalion (less two companies) marched with the brigade to a point on the Ancient Nahrwan Canal, about 4 miles due west of Tekrit, arriving there at 05.00 hours on 5th November. C and D Companies were left to form marching posts at Qantarat-ar-Risasi and Tel Binat respectively. Just after the brigade had halted in the Nahrwan Canal, a Turkish aeroplane flew along it at a very low altitude, evidently looking for troops in the canal. He was fired at with small-arms fire, and it was thought that he must have spotted the brigade, as he turned and flew back directly over it. Every one was expecting bombs or automatic fire which would have done great damage amongst the massed troops in the canal. The Turk, however, flew away, and it was afterwards ascertained that he had seen no troops. The battalion (less three companies) remained in the canal throughout the day, A Company, under Captain Barclay, having been sent nearer the river as escort to a battery which was co-operating with the attack on the right bank.

On 6th November, the attack on the right bank having been successful, the brigade moved to a point on the river opposite Tekrit and bivouacked there.

On 10th November, the Turks having retired to Fatha, the 1st Corps commenced to return to Samarra, arriving there on 12th November without incident. The 21st Brigade again marched down the left bank, picking up C and D Companies of the battalion.

The Move to Akab

On 13th November orders were received that the brigade would march to Akab to relieve the 7th Brigade, and Lieutenant Fleming, with an advance party of twenty men, moved by rail to Beled, and thence marched to Akab, to take over from the 27th Punjabis, who were on the left bank.

On 15th November at 19.00 hours the brigade marched to Imam, a distance of 19 miles, arriving at 05.30 hours the following morning. At 02.00 hours on 17th November the march was resumed and Akab was reached. On arrival the battalion took over the centre section of the Adhaim Bridgehead Defences from 27th Punjabis with A and B Companies, the remainder of the battalion going into camp on the river bank. The remainder of the brigade went into camp on the right bank. On 19th November B Company took over the whole of the centre section, and A Company returned to camp. Captain Strover rejoined the battalion from his Staff appointment on 20th November.

The March up the Adhaim River with the Cavalry Division

At 06.45 hours on 1st December the battalion (less D Company) marched from Akab, as escort to the cart transport of the Cavalry Division to a point on the Adhaim River opposite Satha. Camp was reached at 16.30 hours, the distance being 24 miles. D Company acted as escort to the motor convoy of the Cavalry Division, arriving in camp at 14.30 hours. The Cavalry Division having marched from Sadiyak, down-stream of Akab, arrived in camp after dark.

The following day the battalion, as escort to the Cavalry Division Transport, marched to Chai Khana and put out piquets for the protection of the camp from Arabs. The Cavalry Division attempted to seize the gap in the hills near Band-i-Adhaim, about 5 miles north of camp, but were unable to do so, as the Turks held a strong position on either side of the gap.

The battalion remained in camp for three days, and on 6th December escorted the transport back to the former camp at Satha, B Company acting as escort to the motor convoy. On 8th December the battalion marched for camp at Akab, but on arrival there orders were received to proceed to the right bank and bivouac there for the night, the remainder of the brigade having marched for Baghdad on relief by 34th Brigade. The extra 4 miles at the end of a long march of 24 miles, added to the fact that every one had been looking forward to the camp and hot food ready at Akab, was trying for all ranks.

For the work done while with the Cavalry Division the
G.O.C. wrote thanking all ranks of the battalion for the
good work they had done and complimenting them on their
fine marching.

Move to Baghdad and Basra

On 9th December the battalion marched to Beled railway
station, and the following day entrained for Baghdad, where
they arrived at 12.30 hours, going into bivouac near the
right bank of the river (Tigris).   On 11th December a move
was made to the left bank, and the battalion went into
camp at Hinaidi, where it rejoined the brigade.   On arrival
news was received that the 7th Division were leaving
Mesopotamia for an unknown destination, and speculation
as to where we were going was rife.

The move to Basra commenced on 16th December.
D Company left for Kut by rail and A and B Companies
embarked on two barges.   The following day the remainder
of the battalion embarked on P.51, and, picking up the
barges with A and B Companies, started down-stream.
Kut was reached on 19th December and Headquarters and
C Company transhipped to P.S.97, A and B Companies
remaining on the barges.   The following morning P.S.97,
picking up the two barges, started for Amara, where it
arrived on 23rd December.   The same day the battalion,
less D Company, entrained in two parties and left for Basra.
On 24th December the battalion, less D Company, arrived
at Nahr Umar and went into camp, where D Company had
everything ready.   Lieutenant Fitzgibbon was transferred
to hospital the same day.

The Voyage to Suez

A quiet Christmas was spent in a flooded camp, and on
27th December the battalion embarked on H.T. *Shuja*,
shaking the dust or, in this case, the mud, of Mesopotamia

from their feet. The next day the 121st Pioneers also embarked on the same ship, and on 29th December H.T. *Shuja* sailed for Kuweit Harbour, where she arrived on 30th December, leaving again the following day.

1918

At Mattra on 3rd January, H.T. *Shuja* joined a convoy of five other transports under the escort of H.M.S. *Sapphire* and proceeded under sealed orders, which later disclosed Aden as the next port of call.

Aden was reached on 8th January and Suez a week later. On 15th January the battalion disembarked and, leaving one platoon per company with the heavy kit, entrained for Moascar, which was reached the same day. The battalion went into camp there, and the heavy baggage arrived the next day.

Egypt

While at Moascar, short leave to Cairo, Alexandria and Upper Egypt was freely granted to B.O.s and leave for I.O.s and men was also opened, camps being formed at Cairo and Alexandria. No move was made for the next two months.

On 6th March the division was inspected by the G.O.C.-in-Chief, General Allenby, and on 12th March by H.R.H. The Duke of Connaught, who presented decorations. A party of two I.O.s and seventy-eight I.O.s proceeded on leave to India on 11th March, and one hundred and thirty-seven I.O.R.s surplus to War Establishments were sent to the Base Depôt at Kantara. Captain Strover returned to India on 16th March to give evidence at a Court of Inquiry.

The Move to Palestine

On 25th March the battalion (less two companies) left by road for Kantara, which was reached two days later. The two companies moved a day behind the battalion. From Kantara the move was continued by rail to Ludd, again in two parties. On arrival at Ludd on 29th March, the battalion went into camp at Surafend, where the brigade was being collected.

Trench Warfare North of Jaffa

On 1st April the battalion marched with the brigade to Sarona, a distance of about 10 miles, and, on the following day, the brigade took over the right section of the 7th Division front which extended on the left to the sea. The battalion was in reserve to the Guides, the left battalion of the brigade taking over from the 5th Argyll and Sutherland Highlanders. The battalion was in camp and remained there until 18th April. Lieutenant J. C. S. Hadaway joined the battalion from the Depôt in India on 12th April, being posted to A Company.

On the night 18th/19th April the battalion took over from the 1st Guides with three companies in the front line and B Company in reserve. A Company was on the right of the battalion line, C Company in the centre, and D Company on the left. The enemy trenches were over 1,500 yards away and all was quiet on the battalion front. On 27th April a party of about fifteen Turks, supported by a party with an automatic rifle, attempted a raid on a post held by men of A Company. Some few of the enemy managed to crawl up a nullah to within bombing distance and threw about six bombs, which fell into a machine-gun emplacement held by men of the M.G. Company, killing two and wounding three of them. Fire was at once opened and the enemy retired. A strong patrol was sent out after them, but failed to get into touch. Two men of A Company were wounded.

On the night 2nd/3rd May there was patrol activity in front of A and C Companies. Patrols from C Company were driven in by stronger enemy patrols backed by three or four automatic rifles with which they opened fire on our front line. The fire was returned by our machine-guns and the enemy retired. Strong patrols were sent out, but did not get touch with the enemy again. On A Company front a patrol of about six men was met with and shots were exchanged, one Turk being hit and two Sikhs wounded.

The following night there was again considerable patrol activity on both sides.

On 8th May the battalion was relieved by the 1st Seaforth Highlanders, 19th Brigade, and returned to camp in the Reserve Area, where a draft of one hundred and forty-four I.O.R.s under Lieutenant A. F. Telfer, I.A.R.O., joined the battalion.

While in this area, orders were received to send on a company to the 3/152nd Infantry, which was being formed from companies transferred complete from other battalions. Colonel Fordham decided to send D Company, as they were the last joined, consisting of Kumaonis and Kashmiris, and on 24th May the Company with Captain Brunskill and Lieutenant Hodgkins, left the battalion. The new D Company in the battalion was formed from A Company, i.e. half Sikhs, half Kashmiris.

On 26th May the battalion again moved to the Forward Area, going this time into the left section. This section was divided into the Sisters sub-section and the Valley sub-section. The battalion went into the former and, on 28th and 29th May, acted as carrying party to units of the 28th Brigade in an attack on some enemy posts. The attack was successful; two I.O.R.s of the battalion were killed and nine wounded.

On 30th May the battalion relieved the 51st Sikhs in the Valley sub-section, one company remaining in the Sisters sub-section. On 8th January, as it had been decided to hold the line more thinly in the valley, the battalion took over the portion held by three companies of the 1/8th Gurkha Rifles and the following day, that held by their fourth company. The battalion was now holding a line previously held by two battalions and was consequently very strung out.

During this season there was a lot of malaria amongst all ranks, and Captains Kidd, Bird and Hayes, and Lieutenant Telfer were transferred to hospital. Major L. E. Dening, 3rd Cavalry, Lieutenants Anstey, Cowie, Allen and Second-Lieutenants Price and Billing joined the battalion.

On 16th July the battalion was relieved in the Forward Area and moved to Leicester Wadi on the coast. Here, while making a road, one of a working party of the battalion struck a buried bomb with his pick. The bomb exploded, wounding six men. No one, fortunately, was killed.

On 25th July, Lieutenant-Colonel Fordham was transferred to hospital and Major Dening took over the command of the battalion, which moved, on 31st July, to the Reserve Area.

On 11th August the battalion again moved to the Forward Area, and on 27th August relieved the 2nd Black Watch in the front line trenches. Captain Bird rejoined from hospital on 17th August, Captain Kidd on 28th August and, on 1st September, Lieutenant Stiven joined the battalion. The battalion remained in the front line until 12th September, and, during this tour, one man was killed and nine wounded. Five Turkish deserters came into our trenches at various times during this tour. All were very badly clothed, and stated that they could not get enough to eat and received no pay. On relief the battalion moved to the Reserve Area, where, on 14th September, Lieutenant-Colonel Fordham rejoined from hospital and again took over command. The battalion was now well up to strength, having received drafts to the total of two I.O.s and one hundred and seventy-eight I.O.R.s.

The Attack on Tabsor

On 19th September the battalion was temporarily attached to 19th Brigade and at 04.30 hours the attack on the enemy Tabsor position commenced. The battalion was in reserve with the left column of the brigade, the 28th Punjabis being in the front line and 125th Rifles in support. The attack was a surprise and was carried out practically without opposition. Of the battalion, Captain Anstey, Lieutenant Stiven, and five I.O.R.s were wounded.

The attack broke right through the Turkish position, and those Turks who were not captured hastily retreated. After this attack the battalion rejoined 21st Brigade at about 13.00 hours and marched to Et Tireh.

Action at Falamieh

At 17.00 hours the battalion advanced against the village of Falamieh, coming under fire from enemy machine-guns in the low hills in front of the village, which killed five I.O.R.s and wounded Captain Barclay and twenty-six I.O.R.s of the battalion. As the battalion approached, however, the enemy withdrew and the hills were occupied. As it was by this time nearly dark, it was decided not to push on further through the hills and the brigade put out outposts and bivouacked for the night. Two Turkish officers and six men, all of whom were wounded, were captured.

On the following day the battalion acted as Advanced Guard to the brigade and marched towards Beit Lid. On arrival there at about 17.00 hours it was found that the 19th Brigade were held up by a party of Turks strongly posted in and around the village. The 1st Guides were ordered to occupy Khan Ed Deir and thus threaten the enemy's line of retreat from Beit Lid. The battalion moved in support to the 1st Guides. The enemy, with their retreat thus threatened and pressed by a fresh frontal attack by the 19th Brigade, hurriedly retired. The battalion went on to Messudie with the brigade, where it camped for the night and the following day marched to Samara.

The March up the Coast

On 23rd September the brigade marched to Shueikeh, near Tul Kuram. All along the Tul Kuram valley road was evidence of the havoc wrought by the R.A.F. on the transport of the retreating Turks. The following day the battalion marched with the brigade to Hudeira, and here the battalion was detailed as escort to 91st Heavy Battery (60 Pdrs.) and marched to Zimmarin in rear of 28th Brigade on 26th September. The next march was to Athlit, and on 28th September Haifa was reached, where the battalion rejoined the 21st Brigade.

At Haifa a halt was made until 4th October, when the brigade marched to Acre *en route* for Beirut, which was reached on 10th October. A and B Companies followed under Captain Walker as escort to a composite brigade of artillery and arrived at Beirut a day after the battalion. From here B Company and half C Company under Major Dening marched to Aliye in the hills to guard Turkish dumps and collect salvage. This detachment eventually rejoined the battalion at Tripoli. On 21st October the brigade started to march to Tripoli, which was reached on 28th October. During the march Lieutenant-Colonel Fordham was transferred to hospital on 24th October, and as Major Dening was at Aliye, the command of the battalion devolved on Captain Walker.

Tripoli

On 30th October the brigade moved to a point on the sea coast about 4 miles north of Tripoli, called Ras-el-Lados, and there settled into a camp where it was to remain for

ADVANCE INTO SAMARIA

Miles 10   5   0   10   20 Miles

Situation at 10 p.m. on 18.9.18 as known at GHQ, E.E.F.

MEDITERRANEAN

Heavy guns
in this sector.

Nazareth

Jenin

Sebastie

CORPS

Jaffa

DMC

S.B.

Ramleh

JHAYTOR

Jerusalem (El Kuds)

N.B. Ground reddish
denotes areas in line mes
watch now very lightly held.

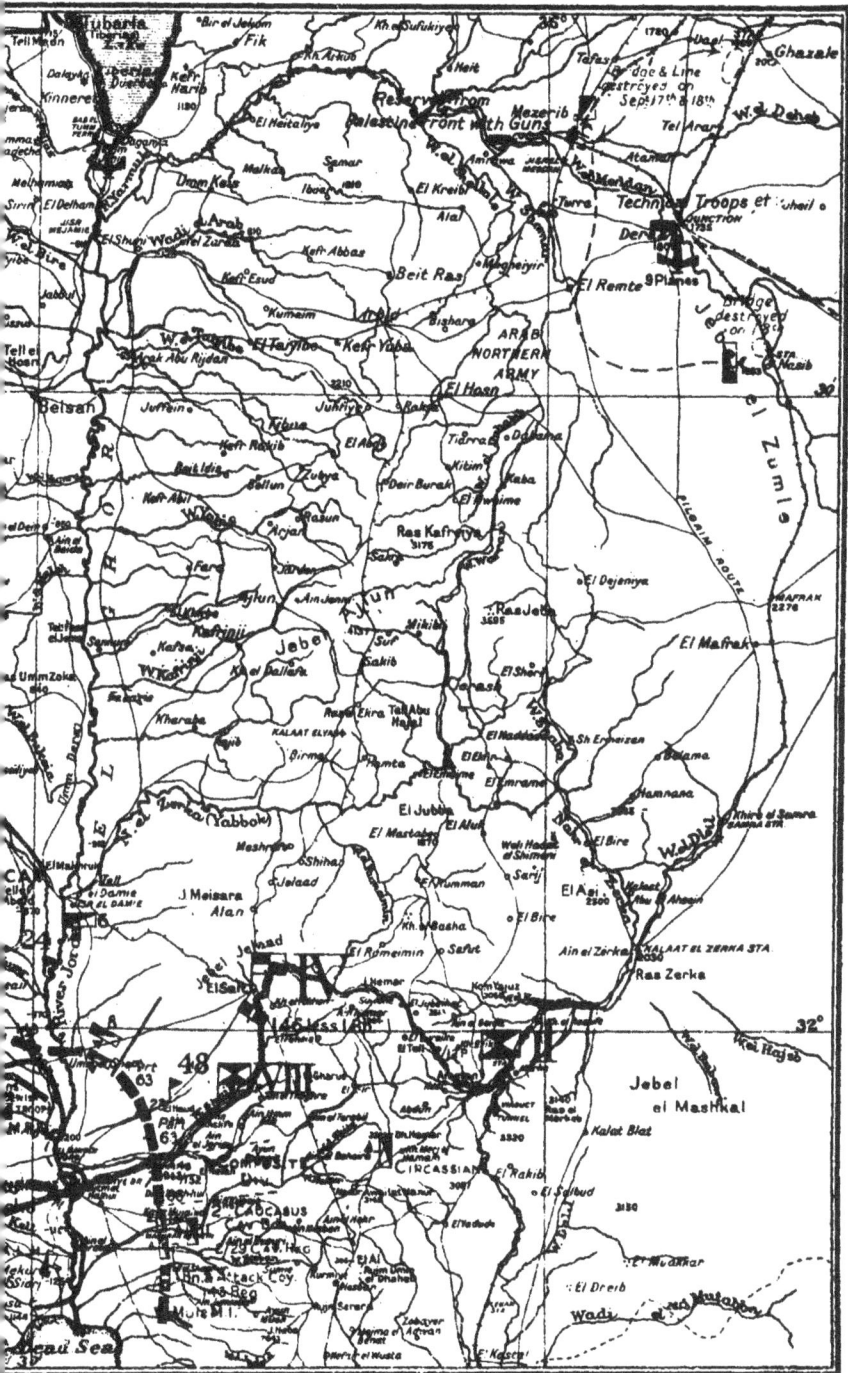

many months. On 31st October an Armistice was concluded with Turkey, by the terms of which hostilities between the Allies and Turkey ceased at 12.00 hours. On the 11th November the Armistice with Germany was signed and the Great War ended.

During November, Lieutenants J. Hunter, J. G. Frith and Second-Lieutenant E. D. B. Legg joined the battalion, and Lieutenant Stiven rejoined from hospital. Lieutenant-Colonel Fordham and Captain Barclay also rejoined from hospital on 25th December.

1919

The battalion remained in the same camp at Ras-el-Lados until March, 1919, when it moved into billets at El Mina, the port of Tripoli. In May, 1919, when the French took over the control of Tripoli, the battalion again moved to a camp on the sea-shore south of Tripoli.

In June, Lieutenant-Colonel Fordham left the battalion to take up a Staff appointment with the 3rd Division, the command of the battalion devolving on Major Dening.

On 29th August, Lieutenant-Colonel C. M. Hawes, D.S.O., was appointed to command the battalion and took over command from Major Hensley of the Guides, who had been in temporary command while Major Dening was away.

The battalion were by this time the only troops left in Tripoli, and every one settled down very comfortably. The men were in a comfortable camp near the sea-shore. The officers were billeted near at hand.

On 18th September the battalion (less B Company) left Tripoli, moved to Beirut, and remained there in camp near the sea until November.

On 11th November the evacuation of Syria by the British commenced, and the battalion marched to Hoshtora in the hills behind Beirut—part of the plan of handing over to the French—returning to Beirut on 28th November, where they were rejoined by B Company from Tripoli. On 4th December the battalion embarked at Beirut for Kantara, arriving there on the 6th December.

There the battalion went into camp with the 7th Division and remained in Kantara until 11th January, 1920.

Captain Bird died in Kantara.

On 16th December one I.O. and seventy-five I.O.R.s, Kumaonis who had been attached to the battalion from the Burma Military Police, returned to India.

1920

On 11th January, 1920, the battalion entrained for Jerusalem and arrived there on the 12th.

The regiment was split up, Headquarters and two companies remaining in Jerusalem, and the other two companies being camped at Ghoraniya, on the shores of the Dead Sea.

On 9th February, Jerusalem experienced the heaviest snowfall for fifty years. The camp awoke in the morning to find itself snowed under. The snow lay to a depth of 39 inches and half covered the tents. The mules in the open were in a wretched state and communication outside the camp almost impossible. Steps were taken at once to clear the camp as much as possible, and also to find, if possible, some cover for men and animals until the snow melted. Luckily, there was a convent school near and the Sisters very kindly placed some empty rooms and a stable at the disposal of the regiment. Owing to this, no harm came to either men or animals, and they remained billeted in comparative comfort until the camp was again clear.

On 22nd March, Headquarters and three companies of the 1st 66th Punjabis arrived at Jerusalem to relieve the regiment ; but on 4th April, when the relief was complete and the regiment was all ready to move to Kantara and return to India, riots broke out in Jerusalem and martial law was proclaimed.

The battalion was on continuous duty in the city during the riots, Captain Fleming with two platoons proceeding to Hebron on the early morning of the 6th April, and arriving just in time to quell a disturbance there.

Orders had been received that the regiment was to sail for India on the H.T. *Berlin* on 15th April, but it seemed doubtful if they would be able to leave Jerusalem at this time. Luckily, however, on 12th April things had so far improved that they were ordered to entrain for Kantara.

Great difficulty was experienced in collecting the regiment and packing up in time to catch the troop train. Captain Fleming and his detachment only arriving at the station an hour or so before the time of departure.

The strength of the battalion at this time was as follows :—

B.Os.	I.O.s	I.O.Rs.
6	15	655

On arrival at Kantara orders were received that there was no room for the regiment on the *Berlin*, and that, therefore, the return to India was postponed. The regiment were naturally bitterly disappointed, as they were, of course, most anxious to return home. However, General Gorringe inspected the battalion on 14th April, and on the facts being put before him promised to do what he could to get the regiment away as soon as possible. He was as good as his word, and orders were received for the regiment to embark on the H.T. *Edouard Woeman* on 20th April. The regiment had the ship to themselves and were most comfortable.

They arrived at Bombay on 3rd May, 1920, and proceeded to Jhelum, where the regimental depôt was stationed.

On arrival at Jhelum all men who could be spared were sent off on two months' war leave.

E

The Zhob

The stay of the regiment in the peace station of Jhelum was short-lived, as on 1st September, 1920, orders were received to move to Murgha in the Zhob, Baluchistan.

On 16th September the regiment railed to Harnai and marched thence to Murgha.

Here the battalion relieved the 111th Mahars and took over the posts of Lakaband, Zarozai and Gurlama, with a detachment also in charge of the dump at Harnai.

In July, 1920, Subadar Major Mota Singh and Subadar Gandha were granted the honorary rank of Lieutenant.

In November, 1920, the regiment marched to Fort Sandeman, relieving the 2/153rd Infantry.

Here Lieutenant-Colonel W. M. Fordham returned from duty on the Staff and took over command of the battalion from Major C. M. Hawes, who had brought the regiment back from Palestine.

In the early part of 1921 the regiment was engaged in the operations which resulted in the re-occupation of the posts of Brunj, Safi, Mir Ali Khel and Moghal Kot, which had been abandoned during the frontier outbreak in 1919.

For these operations, the officers and men who took part have since been awarded the Waziristan medal with clasp 1921–24.

In June, 1921, the regiment marched to Loralai. Whilst here the regiment had a detachment at Killa Saifullah, in addition to the standing detachment at the dump at Harnai.

Colonel W. M. Fordham left the battalion on 16th June, 1921, to take up the appointment of A.A. and Q.M.G. Kohat district.

In June, 1922, Major P. H. McCleverty rejoined the battalion and officiated in command until appointed Commandant of the battalion on 4th November, 1922.

In June, 1922, the regiment again moved to Murgha,

with detachments at Gurlama, Zarozai, Lakaband, Babar, Kapip and Harnai.

During the War, the enlistment of trans-frontier Pathans had ceased, and in 1921 orders were received that in future the composition of the regiment would be :—

One company Sikhs ;

One company Dogras ;

One company Khattaks ; and

One company Punjabi Mohammedans.

The P.M. Company was raised in April, 1921—two platoons were already on the strength at that date, and of the other two platoons one was transferred from the Guides Infantry and one from the 3rd Battalion 152nd Punjabis.

On 1st July, 1921, one platoon of Khattaks was replaced by one platoon of Afridis (Malik Din Khel).

When the reorganization of the Indian army took place in 1921, the battalion was grouped with the 19th, 21st, 22nd and 24th Punjabis and the 40th Pathans instead of with the 21st and 26th Punjabis as heretofore.

In December, 1922, the numbers of all regiments were changed and the 20th D.C.O. Infantry (Brownlow's Punjabis) became The 2nd Battalion, 14th Punjab Regiment (Duke of Cambridge's Own)—(Brownlow's).

Field-Marshal Sir Charles Brownlow, G.C.B., died on 5th April, 1916. Sir Charles raised the regiment in 1857, and always regarded the regiment as his child, and took the greatest interest in everything pertaining to it. His death was deeply regretted by all ranks, who had always regarded him as the true father of the regiment. On 7th August, 1925, Major-General L. C. Dunsterville, C.B., C.S.I., was appointed Colonel of the regiment in succession to Field-Marshal Sir Charles Brownlow, G.C.B.

APPENDICES

OPERATIONS IN WHICH THE REGIMENT TOOK PART,
1908 TO 1922

GREAT WAR

M.E.F. . . . . . 12.10.1914 to 27.12.1917
E.E.F. . . . . . 28.12.1917 to 20.4.1920
Operations, Lower Zhob Posts,
    between . . . . 1.1.1921 to 31.5.1921

COMMANDING OFFICERS

Colonel L. C. Dunsterville . . 20.1.1908 to 21.1.1914
Lieut.-Col. C. Rattray . . 22.1.1914 to 21.1.1918
Lieut.-Col. W. M. Fordham . 22.1.1918 to 16.6.1921
Lieut.-Col. R. S. St. John . 17.6.1921 to 3.11.1922
Lieut.-Col. P. H. McCleverty . 4.11.1922 to 3.12.1926

SUBADAR MAJORS

Name.	Tribe.	Enlisted.	Promoted to Subadar Major.	Pensioned.	Remarks.
Tura Baz Khan .	Khattak	27.7.1882	12.2.1903	31.3.1910	O.B.I. 1st Class with title of Sardur Bahadur. A.D.C. to Commander-in-Chief. Honorary Captain 1.4.1910.
Ali Khan . . .	Khattak	1.5.1889	1.4.1910	9.10.1915	
Masin Khan, I.O.M.	Khattak	3.2.1903	10.10.1915	17.2.1917	Killed in action on 17.2.1917.
Mota Singh . .	Sikh, Ahlu-walia	18.2.1888	18.2.1917	2.10.1920	O.B.I. 2nd Class with title of Bahadur. Honorary Lieut. 1.7.1920.
Amin Gul . .	Adam Khel	4.2.1909	3.10.1920	2.10.1927	Honorary Lieut. 3.10.1927.

STATIONS AT WHICH THE BATTALION HAS BEEN QUARTERED

Station.	Date of Arrival.	Date of Departure.
Jhelum	13.1.1909	4.2.1914
Poona	8.2.1914	30.11.1914
Ferozepore (Depôt)	3.12.1914	14.7.1918
Jhelum (Depôt)	15.7.1918	15.9.1920
Murgha	29.9.1920	24.11.1920
Fort Sandeman	27.11.1920	11.6.1921
Loralai	20.6.1921	2.7.1922
Murgha	5.7.1922	—

LIST OF BRITISH OFFICERS WHO SERVED WITH THE BATTALION DURING THE GREAT WAR

1914

Rank.	Name.	Remarks.
Lieut.-Col.	C. Rattray	Commandant.
Major	W. M. Fordham	Wounded on 17.11.1914.
,,	R. S. St. John	Wounded on 17.11.1914.
,,	R. Ducat	Killed in action on 11.11.1914.
Captain	B. H. Finnis	
,,	P. H. McCleverty	Wounded on 17.11.1914.
,,	E. C. Irwin	
,,	P. D. Saxton	Wounded on 17.11.1914.
,,	C. M. Hawes	Adjutant.
,,	H. J. Daniell	Quartermaster.
Lieutenant	C. H. M. Churchill	
,,	C. T. Burn Murdoch	Wounded on 17.11.1914.
Captain	G. H. Graham, I.M.S.	

1915

Rank.	Name.	Remarks.
Lieut.-Col.	C. Rattray	Assumed Command of Basra Area from 6.4.1915 to 9.4.15. Appointed A.Q.M.G. 12th Division from 16.7.1915.
Major	W. M. Fordham	Invalided to India.
,,	R. S. St. John	Assumed duties of Staff Officer Basra Area from 6.4.1915 to 9.4.1915. Appointed D.A. and Q.M.G. 12th Division (Temp.) from 22.4.1915 to 24.5.1915. Appointed Brigade Major 17th Infy. Brigade from 25.5.1915 to 27.7.1915. Appointed Commandant of the Battalion on 28.7.1915.

Rank.	Name.	Remarks.
Captain	B. H. Finnis	Wounded on 28.9.1915. Invalided to India on 21.10.1915.
,,	P. H. McCleverty	Wounded (slight) on 28.9.1915.
,,	E. C. Irwin	
,,	P. D. Saxton	Invalided to India.
,,	C. C. Stewart	Joined M.E.F. on 18.5.1915. Appointed Staff Captain 16th Infy. Brigade on 11.9.1915. Killed in action on 22.11.1915.
Captain	C. M. Hawes	Appointed Asst. Provost-Marshal 12th Division from 22.4.1915 to 29.6.1915. Appointed Assistant to the Post Comdt. for Political duties from 30.6.1915 to 6.7.1915. Appointed Post Commandant L. of C. from 9.12.1915.
,,	H. J. Daniell	Appointed Staff Captain 16th Inf. Brigade from 22.11.1915.
Lieutenant	C. H. M. Churchill	Appointed Adjutant 1.6.1915.
,,	C. T. Burn Murdoch	Appointed Quartermaster 22.11.1915.

1916

Rank.	Name.	Remarks.
Major (A/Lieut.-Col.)	W. M. Fordham	Rejoined M.E.F. on 12.4.1916 and assumed Command of the Battalion on 27.4.1916.
Major	R. S. St. John	Appointed Commandant Amara from 13.12.1915 to 8.3.1916. Appointed A.Q.M.G.L. O/C. Headquarters Basra from 8.3.1916.
Captain	B. H. Finnis	Rejoined M.E.F. on 27.1.1916. Offg. Commandant from 8.3.1916 to 27.4.1916.

Rank.	Name.	Remarks.
Captain	P. H. McCleverty	
,,	E. C. Irwin	Proceeded to East Africa for Service with 40th Pathans on 5.4.1916. Killed in action in East Africa on 19.7.1918.
,,	C. M. Hawes	Returned to India for Duty at Depôt on 6.9.1916.
,,	H. J. Daniell	Taken prisoner of war at Kut on 29.4.1916. Died of disease on 19.8.1916.
,,	C. H. M. Churchill	Adjutant.
Lieutenant	C. T. Burn Murdoch	Appointed Station Staff Officer Amara from 13.12.1915 to 2.9.16. Returned to India for Duty at Depôt on 6.9.1916. Joined South Waziristan Militia. Killed in retreat from Wana on 30.5.1919.
2nd-Lieut.	L. Hayes, I.A.R.O.	Joined M.E.F. on 10.1.1916. Appointed Quartermaster on 7.9.1916.
,,	L. B. FitzGibbon, I.A.R.O.	Joined M.E.F. on 27.4.1916.
Captain	C. H. Brock, I.A.R.O.	Joined M.E.F. on 27.6.1916. Appointed Adjutant Indian Advance Depôt Amara.
,,	F. W. Morton-Marshall, 130th Baluchis	Joined M.E.F. on 27.6.1916. Joined Battalion on 2.9.1916.
Lieutenant	G. R. Kidd	Joined M.E.F. on 27.7.1916. Adjutant.
Lieutenant	T. Fleming, I.A.R.O.	Joined M.E.F. on 27.7.1916. Appointed Brigade Transport Officer from 17.9.1916 to 21.2.1917.
2nd-Lieut.	F. Barclay, I.A.R.O.	Joined the Battalion from 27th Punjabis on 22.7.1916.
,,	L. G. Burgess, I.A.R.O.	Joined M.E.F. on 22.10.1916.
,,	E. L. F. Berkeley, I.A.R.O.	Joined M.E.F. on 30.11.16.
Lieutenant	V. N. Agate, I.M.S.	Joined the Battalion on 28.3.1916.

1917

Rank.	Name.	Remarks.
Lieut.-Col.	W. M. Fordham	
Major	R. S. St. John	Proceeded to India on 8.6.1917. Appointed Embarkation Commandant, Bombay.
Captain	B. H. Finnis	Invalided to India on 9.1.1917.
,,	P. H. McCleverty	Invalided to India on 11.1.1917.
,,	C. M. Hawes	Rejoined M.E.F. on 9.4.1917.
(A/Major)		Awarded Order of the White Eagle, 5th Class (with Swords). by H.M. the King of Serbia. To be acting Major from 21.5.1917. Appointed G.S.O. III, 17th Division from 12.9.1917.
Captain	C. H. M. Churchill	Killed in action on 17.2.1917.
,,	G. R. Kidd	Adjutant.
,,	L. Hayes, I.A.R.O.	Awarded Military Cross on 21.4.1917.
Lieutenant	L. B. FitzGibbon, I.A.R.O.	
Captain	F. W. Morton-Marshall, 130th Baluchis	Invalided to India on 25.5.1917.
Lieutenant	T. Fleming	Mentioned in Despatches on 12.10.1917.
,,	F. Barclay, I.A.R.O.	
2nd Lieut.	L. G. Burgess, I.A.R.O.	Killed in action on 17.2.1917.
,,	E. L. F. Berkeley, I.A.R.O.	Invalided to India on 9.6.1917.
,,	J. H. B. B. Hart, 40th Pathans	Joined M.E.F. on 20.3.1917. Invalided to India on 6.7.1917.
,,	W. Roan, I.A.R.O.	Joined M.E.F. on 10.1.1917. Invalided to India on 26.2.1917. Rejoined M.E.F. on 11.10.1917. Permanently transferred to Railway Department in Mesopotamia on 24.1.1918.
Lieutenant	N. F. Hodgkins, 80th Carnatic Infantry	Joined M.E.F. on 5.2.1917.

Rank.	Name.	Remarks.
Lieutenant	G. H. Raschen, 26th Punjabis	Joined M.E.F. on 7.3.1917. Wounded on 21.4.1917. Invalided to India on 5.5.1917.
Captain	E. K. Bird, 29th Punjabis	Joined M.E.F. on 20.4.1917.
,,	W. G. Strover, 5th Infantry	Joined M.E.F. on 30.4.1917. Took over duties of Staff Captain 21st Infantry Brigade on 8.6.1917. Appointed G.S.O. III, 1st Corps 12.9.1917 to 20.11.1917.
Lieutenant	E. T. O. Sullivan, 66th Punjabis	Joined M.E.F. on 14.5.1917.
Captain	H. R. O. Walker, 25th Punjabis	Joined M.E.F. on 3.9.1917.
,,	B. A. S. Brunskill, 79th Carnatic Infantry	Joined M.E.F. on 15.7.1917.
Lieutenant	V. N. Agate, I.M.S.	Transferred to Basra for duty on 15.6.1917.
,,	G. A. Khan, I.M.S.	Joined the Battalion on 1.7.1917.

Captain P. W. Elliott, who was medically unfit for service, did yeoman work for the Regiment in command of the Depôt.

1918
BATTALION LANDED AT SUEZ ON 15.1.18

Rank.	Name.	Remarks.
Lieut.-Col.	W. M. Fordham	
Major	C. M. Hawes	Appointed Brigade Major 7th Infy. Brigade on 21.1.1918.
Captain	G. R. Kidd	Adjutant.
,,	L. Hayes, I.A.R.O.	Quartermaster.
Lieutenant (A/Capt.)	T. Fleming, I.A.R.O.	
Lieutenant	L. B. Fitzgibbon, I.A.R.O.	Invalided to India 21.1.1918.

Rank.	Name.	Remarks.
Lieutenant (A/Capt.)	F. Barclay, I.A.R.O.	Wounded on 19.9.1918.
Captain	B. A. S. Brunskill, 79th Carnatic Infantry	Transferred to 3/152nd Punjabis on 25.5.1918.
Lieutenant	N. F. Hodgkins, 80th Carnatic Infantry	Transferred to 3/152nd Punjabis on 25.5.1918.
Captain	E. K. Bird, 29th Punjabis	
,,	W. G. Strover, 5th Infantry	Returned to India on 16.3.1918.
Lieutenant	E. T. O'Sullivan, 66th Punjabis	
Captain	H. R. O. Walker, 25th Punjabis	Posted to his own Unit.
Lieutenant	J. C. S. Hadaway	Joined E.E.F. on 16.3.1918. Offg. Adjutant 26.7.1918 to 17.8.1918.
,,	J. Hunter, 71st Punjabis (I.A.R.O.)	Joined E.E.F. on 27.4.1918.
,,	E. R. B. Upton, I.A.R.O.	
,,	D. Anstey	Wounded and remained on Duty on 19.9.1918. Mentioned in Despatches.
,,	C. J. Price	
,,	G. A. Allen	Joined E.E.F. on 29.6.1918. Transferred to 2nd Leicester Regiment on 24.12.1918.
Lieutenant	G. A. Khan, I.M.S.	Wounded and remained on Duty on 20.9.1918.

LIST OF INDIAN OFFICERS SERVED WITH THE BATTALION DURING THE GREAT WAR

1914

Rank.	Name.	Remarks.
Sub. Major	Ali Khan	
Subadar	Masin Khan	
,,	Mota Singh	
,,	Saleh Khan	
,,	Imat Khan	Wounded on 11.11.1914. Invalided to India on 29.11.1914.
,,	Ganda	Wounded on 11.11.1914. Invalided to India on 29.11.1914.
,,	Kapura	
,,	Kala Singh	
,,	Barhawan	
Jemadar	Sant Singh	
,,	Pala Singh	
,,	Amin Gul	
,,	Kashmir Singh	
,,	Khan	
,,	Chakand	
,,	Mawaz Khan	
,,	Wali Khan	Invalided to India on 30.12.1914.
,,	Jhanda Singh	
,,	Khushala	
,,	Hassan Khan	Joined M.E.F. on 14.12.14.

1915

Rank.	Name.	Remarks.
Sub. Major	Ali Khan	Returned to India 18.7.1915.
Subadar	Masin Khan	Wounded 28.9.1915. Awarded I.O.M. 28.9.15. Promoted Subadar Major 10.10.1915.
,,	Mota Singh	
,,	Saleh Khan	Returned to India 24.8.1915.
,,	Kapura	Wounded 28.9.1915. Died of disease at Basra on 18.12.1915.
,,	Kala Singh	Returned to India 18.7.1915.
,,	Sant Singh	Promoted Subadar 18.7.1915.
,,	Amin Gul	,, ,, 15.8.1915.
,,	Barhawan	
,,	Kashmir Singh	Wounded 28.9.1915. Promoted Subadar 12.12.1915.
Jemadar	Pala Singh	Returned to India 15.5.1915.
,,	Khan	
,,	Chakand	Returned to India 15.5.1915.
,,	Mawaz Khan	Invalided to India 3.5.1915.
,,	Hassan Khan	
,,	Jhanda Singh	
,,	Natha Singh	Promoted Jemadar 18.12.1915.
,,	Ladha Singh	,, ,, 16.5.1915.
,,	Hazrat Shah	,, ,, 10.4.1915. Wounded 28.9.1915.
,,	Aslam	Promoted Jemadar 1.6.1915. Wounded and died of wounds on 28.9.1915.
,,	Udham Singh	Joined M.E.F. 27.9.1915.
,,	Khushala	
,,	Mian Din	
,,	Habib Khan	
,,	Zar Khan	

1916

Rank.	Name.	Remarks.
Sub. Major	Masin Khan, I.O.M.	
Subadar	Mota Singh	
,,	Sant Singh	
,,	Amin Gul	Transferred to East Africa for Service with 40th Pathans on 5.4.1916.
,,	Kashmir Singh	
,,	Barhawan	
,,	Ghulam Rasul	Kashmiri. Joined M.E.F. 22.10.1916.
,,	Mohamed Khan	Kashmiri. Joined M.E.F. 22.10.1916.
Jemadar	Khan	Transferred to East Africa for Service with 40th Pathans on 5.4.1916.
,,	Hassan Khan	Invalided to India on 12.7.1916.
,,	Jhanda Singh	
,,	Natha Singh	
,,	Ladha Singh	
,,	Hazrat Shah	Transferred to East Africa for Service with 40th Pathans on 5.4.1916.
,,	Mian Din	Invalided to India on 4.4.1916.
,,	Alam Khan	Promoted Jemadar 18.5.1916. Invalided to India 6.12.1916.
,,	Zar Khan	Transferred to East Africa for Service with 40th Pathans on 5.4.1916.
,,	Said Gul	Promoted Jemadar 4.10.1916.
,,	Udham Singh	
,,	Khushala	
,,	Habib Khan	
,,	Mohamed Din	Kashmiri. Joined M.E.F. 22.10.1916. Invalided to India 11.12.1916.
,,	Fazal Ilahi	Kashmiri. Joined M.E.F. 22.10.1916. Invalided to India 16.12.1916.

1917

Rank.	Name.	Remarks.
Sub. Major	Masin Khan, I.O.M.	Killed in action 17.2.1917.
Subadar	Mota Singh	Promoted Subadar Major 18.2.1917.
,,	Sant Singh	Invalided to India 28.5.1917.
,,	Kashmir Singh	Wounded 17.2.1917.
,,	Barhawan	
,,	Said Gul	Promoted Subadar 5.5.1917. Wounded on 12.2.1917. Invalided to India 19.3.1917.
,,	Ghulam Rasul	Kashmiri. Invalided to India 5.5.1917.
,,	Mohamed Khan	Kashmiri. Wounded on 17.2.1917.
,,	Ladha Singh	Promoted Subadar 13.5.1917.
,,	Habib Khan	
,,	Niaz Ali	Kashmiri. Joined M.E.F. 30.6.1917.
Jemadar	Natha Singh	Wounded 17.2.1917. Invalided to India 2.4.1917.
,,	Sansaru	Joined M.E.F. 10.4.1917.
,,	Udham Singh	Wounded 17.2.1917.
,,	Lakha Singh	Promoted Jemadar 18.2.1917.
,,	Khushala	
,,	Jhanda Singh	Killed in action 17.2.1917.
,,	Mustaqim	Kashmiri. Joined M.E.F. 10.4.1917.
,,	Mohd Zaman Khan	Kashmiri. Joined M.E.F. 27.5.1917.
,,	Niaz Gul	Joined M.E.F. 6.1.1917. Wounded 17.2.1917.
,,	Makhmad	Promoted Jemadar 1.1.1917.
,,	Sant Singh	,, ,, 18.2.1917.
,,	Sharif	,, ,, ,,
,,	Mawaz Khan	Rejoined M.E.F. 7.3.1917. Invalided to India 5.5.1917.
Subadar	Mohd Bakhsh	Burma Military Police. Joined M.E.F. 9.4.1917. Returned to India 5.11.1917.
,,	Daulat Singh	B.M.P. Joined M.E.F. 10.4.1917.
,,	Uchhab Singh	,, ,, ,, 22.7.1917.
Jemadar	Fazal Dad Khan	,, ,, ,, 23.8.1917.
,,	Nain Singh Chand	,, ,, ,, 3.9.1917.

F

1918

BATTALION LANDED AT SUEZ ON 15.1.18

Rank.	Name.	Remarks
Sub. Major	Mota Singh	
Subadar	Kashmir Singh	
,,	Barhawan	Returned to India 21.1.1918.
,,	Said Gul	
,,	Mohd Khan	Kashmiri. Transferred to 3/152nd Punjabis 25.5.1918.
,,	Ladha Singh	Returned to India 14.1.1918.
,,	Habib Khan	,, ,, 16.11.1918.
,,	Niaz Ali	Kashmiri.
,,	Makhmad	
,,	Khushala	Awarded O.B.I. 2nd Class. Invalided to India 7.11.1918.
,,	Udham Singh	Promoted Subadar 20.10.1918.
,,	Sharif	,, ,, 16.11.1918.
Jemadar	Sansaru	
,,	Alam Khan	
,,	Sant Singh	Invalided to India 10.8.1918.
,,	Niaz Gul	Returned to India 7.11.1918.
,,	Lakha Singh	
,,	Mewa Singh, I.O.M.	
,,	Nur Khan	Promoted Jemadar 7.11.1918.
,,	Jagtu	,, ,, 17.9.1918.
,,	Dharam Singh	,, ,, 23.10.1918.
,,	Mohd Zaman Khan	Kashmiri.
Subadar	Daulat Singh	B.M.P.
,,	Uchhab Singh	B.M.P. Invalided to India 10.8.1918.
Jemadar	Fazal Dad Khan	B.M.P. Invalided to India 7.11.1918.
,,	Nain Singh Chand	B.M.P. Invalided to India 13.1.1918.

LIST OF B.O.s, I.O.s, N.C.O.s, MEN AND FOLLOWERS DIED OF WOUNDS AND KILLED IN ACTION

Regtl. No.	Rank.	Name.	Remarks.
	Major	R. Ducat	
	,,	F. L. Hughes	
	Captain	C. H. M. Churchill	
	,,	H. C. Rome	
	,,	E. C. Irwin	
	Lieutenant	C. T. Burn-Murdoch	
	2nd-Lieut.	L. G. Burgess, I.A.R.O.	
	Sub. Major	Masin Khan	
	Jemadar	Aslam	
	,,	Jhanda Singh	
29	Havildar	Sher Madi	
4898	,,	Hoshnak	
813	,,	Ram Dass	
509	,,	Mainga	
4724	,,	Abdul Rahman	
4555	Col. Hav.	Hukam Singh	
68	Havildar	Mir Afzal Khan	
100	,,	Chattar Singh	
1672	,,	Sultan	
684	,,	Billo	
456	,,	Dhela	
1267	,,	Sham Singh	
3035	,,	Karim Bakhsh	
534	Naik	Prem Singh	
1331	,,	Mangtu	
3131	,,	Rahmat Khan	
450	,,	Natha Singh	
1282	,,	Wakil Singh	
998	,,	Bhola Singh	
1058	,,	Radhu	
1697	,,	Babu Ram	
175	,,	Gulaba	
1408	,,	Gul Bayan	
935	,,	Harnam Singh	
1760	Sepoy	Ghafar	
773	,,	Mangoo	
1589	,,	Labhoo	

Regtl. No.	Rank.	Name.	Remarks.
1889	Sepoy	Sain	
1778	,,	Sherin Khan	
1536	,,	Kishan Singh	
1728	,,	Hazara Singh	
1864	,,	Hari Singh	
1932	,,	Dalip Singh	
970	,,	Prab Dayal	
1705	,,	Alim Khan	
950	,,	Jawahir Singh	
1607	,,	Bhagtu	
892	,,	Sabz Singh	
1350	Bugler	Lakhia	
1206	Sepoy	Gitan	
1608	,,	Awal Khan	
1183	,,	Sherin	
1463	,,	Jalat Khan	
1846	,,	Gulaba	
1613	,,	Sher Hasan	
1284	L/Naik	Nahar Singh	
1195	Sepoy	Gul Sharaf	
1146	,,	Dalip Singh	
651	,,	Giyana	
1283	L/Naik	UdhamSingh	
907	Sepoy	Ran Singh	
1940	,,	Gul Khan	
1658	,,	Harnam Singh	
2033	,,	Makhmad Yusaf	
1691	,,	Harnam Singh	
928	,,	Hazara Singh	
1257	,,	Payo Gul	
2235	,,	Udham Singh	
2092	,,	Mian Mohammad Khan	
2185	,,	Sham Singh	
2202	,,	Sudha Singh	
2077	,,	Kaura	
522	,,	Wakil	
1994	,,	Sundar Singh	
3210	,,	Piran Ditta	
1732	,,	Nand Singh	
1975	,,	Banta Singh	

Regtl. No.	Rank.	Name.	Remarks.
2541	Sepoy	Lachman Singh	
2800	,,	Sundar Singh	
1401	L/Naik	Kore Singh	
2388	Sepoy	Hukam Singh	
1995	,,	Sant Singh	
1274	L/Naik	Hari Singh	
1145	,,	Jassa Singh	
2253	Sepoy	Sant Singh	
1909	,,	Lal Singh	
2238	,,	Mehr Singh	
1557	L/Naik	Labh Singh	
2364	Sepoy	Sharam Singh	
2242	,,	Mausim	
2699	,,	Fazlai Anar	
2352	,,	Polo	
3248	,,	Ahmed Din	
2373	,,	Mathra	
2265	,,	Munshi	
1768	,,	Sobha	
2083	,,	Laddu	
2742	,,	Tulsi Ram	
1465	L/Naik	Makar Din	
1900	Sepoy	Zarin Khan	
2600	,,	Shah Bahram	
2000	,,	Saifal	
1586	L/Naik	Shah Alam Khan	
2199	Sepoy	Abdul Rahman	
3025	,,	Ahmed Din	
3064	,,	Jalal Din	
3117	,,	Abdullah Khan	
3096	,,	Hassan Din	
1482	,,	Shah Baz	21st Punjabis attached.
1860	,,	Shah Baz	,, ,, ,,
2767	,,	Multan Singh	
2267	,,	Mian Singh	
1935	,,	Dalip Singh	
2720	,,	Kesar Singh	
3167	,,	Allah Ditta	
4127	,,	Jalal Din	
3079	,,	Allah Lok	
1462	L/Naik	Sawal	

Regtl. No.	Rank.	Name.	Remarks.
1755	Sepoy	Nandoo	
1766	,,	Awal Khan	
1346	,,	Mehr Wali	
2467	,,	Nur Mohamad	
2037	,,	Gul Hassan	
2568	,,	Khairan	
3192	,,	Mohamad Sharif	
1689	,,	Hazara Singh	
1784	,,	Dhanna Singh	
1855	,,	Nal Singh	
3055	,,	Khusi Mohamad	
4280	,,	Nabi Bakhsh	
4495	,,	Wazir Khan	
2504	,,	Roli	
1230	,,	Indar Singh	
2560	,,	Rasil Singh	
1781	,,	Taj-ud-Din	
1692	,,	Sohan Singh	
2625	,,	Makhai Din	
2181	,,	Sultan Singh	
1411	,,	Indar Singh	21st Punjabis attached.
1960	,,	Diwan Singh	
2241	,,	Bhukhoo	
1810	,,	Jai Karn	
2793	,,	Phangan	
2201	,,	Santa Singh	
2245	,,	Mohan Singh	B.M.P. attached.
1772	L/Naik	Khaliq Dad	
2206	,,	Hubab Shah	
2005	Sepoy	Gul Khasan	
2050	,,	Tor Khan	
638	,,	Jagat Singh	21st Punjabis attached.
2086	,,	Balanda	
401	Bhisti	Allah Din	
106	Sweeper	Jhandu	

LIST OF B.O.s, I.O.s, N.C.O.s, MEN AND FOLLOWERS DIED OF DISEASE ON FIELD SERVICE

Regtl. No.	Rank.	Name.	Remarks.
	Captain	H. J. Daniel	Whilst prisoner of war.
	,,	E. K. Bird	29th Punjabis attached.
	Subadar	Kapura	
4802	Havildar	Kehar Singh	
699	,,	Lal Singh	
381	Naik	Haidar Khan	B.M.P. attached.
1236	Sepoy	Dalel Singh	
1393	,,	Mirabas	
1294	,,	Kishan Singh	
1250	,,	Wazir Chand	
1530	,,	Sher Zada	
653	L/Naik	Lal Mir	
1706	Sepoy	Sher Jang	
1187	,,	Atta Mohamad	
1713	,,	Gaji	
688	,,	Jaimal Singh	
1852	,,	Ali Sher	
1860	,,	Mehrba Din	
2176	,,	Lal Singh	
2136	,,	Badal Bang	
1417	,,	Feroze Khan	
1800	,,	Abdullah Khan	
2038	,,	Nasib Singh	
4592	,,	Atta Mohammad	
2356	,,	Rasil Singh	
1855	,,	Ali Akhmad	21st Punjabis attached.
3920	,,	Noor Alam	
943	,,	Khan Zaman	B.M.P. attached.
2228	,,	Shib Singh	B.M.P. attached.
1934	,,	Milkhi	
4442	,,	Saddar Din	
1795	,,	Shimroz	21st Punjabis attached.
2947	,,	Ruoa Dhar	B.M.P. attached.
2964	,,	Kalu Chand	B.M.P. attached.
2704	,,	Lachman Singh	B.M.P. attached.
1116	,,	Sher Khan	21st Punjabis attached.
973	,,	Asa Singh	
2318	,,	Jagan Nath	

Regtl. No.	Rank.	Name.	Remarks.
4612	Sepoy	Natha Singh	
4249	,,	Rala Singh	
1773	T/Naik	Wali Jang	
1714	L/Naik	Mehr Chand	
2866	Sepoy	Wasaf Shah	
1581	,,	Hamid Ullah	21st Punjabis attached.
2398	,,	Nam Singh	
2072	,,	Sukh Lal	
392	L/Naik	Mohamad Mir	21st Punjabis attached.
2044	Sepoy	Sunko	
2288	,,	Nur Baz	
3590	,,	Makhan Khan	
3099	,,	Mohamad Din	
	Bhisti	Isar	
	,,	Chajju	

The War Memorial, to the Memory of the B.O.'s, I.O.'s and Men of the Battalion who were killed or died on service during the War 1914–1918, was subscribed for by the Battalion and was unveiled at Ferozepore on the 3rd December 1923, by General Sir William Birdwood, G.C.B., G.C.M.G., K.C.S.I., C.I.E., D.S.O., the G.O.C.-in-C. Northern Command.

THE WAR MEMORIAL, FEROZEPORE

HONOURS AND REWARDS GRANTED DURING THE GREAT WAR 1914–1918

Regtl. No.	Rank.	Name.	Remarks.
		D.S.O.	
	Lieut.-Col.	R. S. St. John	
	Major	C. M. Hawes	
		MILITARY CROSS	
	Captain	B. A. S. Brunskill	3/152nd Punjabis attached.
	,,	P. D. Saxton	
	Lieut.	L. Hayes	
	Subadar	Mohamed Khan	3/152nd Punjabis attached.
		I.O.M.	
	A/Sub. Maj.	Masin Khan	
204	Havildar	Mewa Singh	
822	Bug.-Major	Surain Singh	
1058	L/Naik	Radhu	
1689	Sepoy	Hazara Singh	
2158	L/Naik	Churu	
2626	Sepoy	Makhmad Ali	
3004	Naik	Ramzan	3/152nd Punjabis attached.
		FOREIGN ORDERS	
	Major	R. S. St. John	By H.M. The King of Serbia. Order of Karageorge, 4th Class, with Swords.
	Captain	C. M. Hawes	By H.M. The King of Serbia. Order of White Eagle, 5th Class, with Swords.

Regtl. No.	Rank.	Name.	Remarks.
		I.D.S.M.	
1483	L/Naik	Kirpa	
1937	Sepoy	Bhima	
1576	,,	Bachittar	
1099	L/Naik	Ghulam Haidar	
370	Naik	Sher Ali	
		O.B.I.	
	Subadar	Khushala	
		FOREIGN MEDALS	
998	Naik	Bhola Singh	Gold. By H.M. The King of Serbia.
1142	L/Naik	Mehar Singh	Silver. By H.M. The King of Serbia.
		ROYAL HUMANE SOCIETY MEDAL	
1590	Sepoy	Achhar Singh	
		MENTIONED IN DESPATCHES	
	Major	R. S. St. John	
	Lieut.-Col.	W. M. Fordham	
	Major	C. M. Hawes	
	Captain	P. D. Saxton	
	,,	G. R. Kidd	
	Lieutenant	D. Anstey	
	,,	T. Fleming	
	Captain	C. C. Stewart	
	A/Sub. Maj.	Masin Khan	
	Subadar	Mota Singh	
	,,	Barhawan	
204	Havildar	Mewa Singh	
	Jemadar	Sharif	
	Subadar	Amin Gul	
484	Havildar	Ganda Singh	
1753	A/Naik	Gopal Singh	
1576	Sepoy	Bachittar	
2158	,,	Churu	

Regtl. No.	Rank.	Name.	Remarks.

MENTIONED IN DESPATCHES—continued.

Regtl. No.	Rank.	Name.	Remarks.
1662	Sepoy	Surain Singh	
1954	,,	Ganga Ram	
617	Havildar	Mangal Singh	
1483	L/Naik	Kirpa	
1099	,,	Ghulam Haidar	
1058	,,	Radhu	
1937	Sepoy	Bhima	
822	Bug.-Major	Surain Singh	
1689	Sepoy	Hazara Singh	

INDIAN OFFICERS AWARDED O.B.I. AND I.O.M.— FROM RAISING OF THE REGIMENT TO 1922

Date.	Rank.	Name.	Remarks.
April, 1863	Subadar	Omrao Missar	Bahadur. O.B.I. 2nd Class.
April, 1865	Sub. Maj.	Jai Singh	Bahadur. ,, ,, ,,
July, 1872	,, ,,	Jai Singh	Sirdar Bahadur. O.B.I. 1st Class.
April, 1877	Subadar	Nihal Singh	Bahadur. O.B.I. 2nd Class.
,, ,,	,,	Maula Dad	I.O.M. 2nd Class.
,, ,,	,,	Mir Mohamad	I.O.M. 3rd Class.
,, ,,	,,	Chuttar Singh	,, ,, ,,
,, ,,	Jemadar	Mir Alum	,, ,, ,,
July, 1878	Subadar	Maula Dad	I.O.M. 1st Class.
April, 1879	,,	Maula Dad	Bahadur. O.B.I. 2nd Class.
July, 1882	Sub.-Maj.	Maula Dad	Sirdar Bahadur. O.B.I. 1st Class.
July, 1885	,,	Maula Dad	Sirdar Bahadur. C.I.E.
July, 1885	Jemadar	Binda	Bahadur. O.B.I. 2nd Class.
Jan., 1886	Subadar	Zaman Khan	Bahadur. ,, ,, ,,
April, 1887	,,	Zaman Khan	Sirdar Bahadur. O.B.I. 1st Class.
,, ,,	,,	Arsala Khan	,, ,, ,, ,,
,, ,,	Jemadar	Alim Khan	Khan Sahib.
Jan., 1898	Sub. Maj.	Arbela	Bahadur. O.B.I. 2nd Class.
July, 1898	Subadar	Hassan Khan	I.O.M. 3rd Class.
July, 1898	Jemadar	Abdulla	,, ,, ,,
Oct., 1901	Subadar	Tura Baz Khan	Bahadur. O.B.I. 2nd Class.
Jan., 1903	Sub. Maj.	Arbela	Sirdar Bahadur. O.B.I. 1st Class.
,, ,,	Subadar	Tura Baz Khan	,, ,, ,, ,,
Oct., 1906	,,	Jai Dial	Bahadur. O.B.I. 2nd Class.
Jan., 1909	Jemadar	Abdulla	,, O.B.I. 2nd Class.
,, 1912	Subadar	Salih Khan	,, ,, ,, ,,
,, ,,	,,	Dayal Singh	,, ,, ,, ,,
,, 1914	,,	Moti	,, ,, ,, ,,
July, 1914	,,	Unkar Singh	,, ,, ,, ,,
Oct., 1919	,,	Khushala	,, ,, ,, ,,
Jan., 1920	Sub. Maj.	Mota Singh	,, ,, ,, ,,
,, 1920	Subadar	Ganda	,, ,, ,, ,,

LIST OF OFFICERS WHO HAVE SERVED WITH THE 20TH D.C.O. INFANTRY UP TO END OF 1922

Name.	Rank.	Remarks.
Allen, G. A.	2nd Lieut.	Attached to the Battalion for Active Service E.E.F., 29.6.1918. Transferred to 2nd Liecester Regiment on 24.12.1918.
Anstey, D.	Lieutenant	Attached to the Battalion for Active Service E.E.F. 20.8.1918. Mentioned in Despatches 19.9.1918. Transferred to I.A.S.C. 1922.
Archer, W. A.	Lieutenant	Joined the Battalion on 10.5.1922. Demobilised 9.8.1922.
Armitage, K. L. F., I.A.R.O.	Lieutenant	Attached to the Battalion 1.5.1916.
Ballard, V., I.A.R.O.	2nd Lieut.	Attached to the Battalion 8.11.1917 and transferred to the S. and T. Department in 1919.
Barclay, F., I.A.R.O., 27th Punjabis	Lieutenant	Attached to the Battalion for Active Service M.E.F. 22.7.1916 to 27.12.1917. E.E.F. 28.12.1917. Demobilised 1.4.1919.
Berkeley, E. L. F., I.A.R.O.	2nd Lieut.	Attached to the Battalion for Active Service on 30.11.1916 and Invalided to India on 9.6.1917.
Billing, E. W.	Lieutenant	Attached to the Battalion for Active Service on 4.11.1917. Resigned on 7.6.1920.
Bird, E. K., 29th Punjabis	Captain	Attached to the Battalion for Active Service M.E.F. 20.4.1917 to 27.12.1917, E.E.F. 28.12.1917. Died of disease on 27.9.1919.
Brock, C. H., I.A.R.O.	Captain	Attached to the Battalion 23.6.1916, and appointed Adjutant Indian Advance Depôt, Amara.

Name.	Rank.	Remarks.
Boyce, T. W., M.C., M.M.	Lieutenant	Joined the Battalion as Adjutant from 71/111th Mahars on 7.12.1922.
Brown, G.	Lieutenant	Joined the Battalion on 13.11.1921.
Brownlow, C. C. S.	Lieutenant	Invalided out of the Service 6.8.1912.
Brunskill, B. A. S., 79th Carnatic Infantry	Captain	Attached to the Battalion for Active Service M.E.F. 15.7.1917 to 27.12.1917. E.E.F. 27.12.1917. Transferred to 3/152nd Punjabis in the field on 25.5.1918. Rejoined the Battalion on 1.5.1921 and transferred to 2/39th Garhwal Rifles 24.11.1921.
Burgess, L. G., I.A.R.O.	2nd Lieut.	Attached to the Battalion for Active Service M.E.F. 22.10.1916 and killed in action on 17.2.1917.
Burn-Murdoch, C. T.	Lieutenant	Joined the Battalion at Jhelum in 1913 and served with the Battalion on Active Service. M.E.F. from 12.10.1914 to 6.9.1916. Killed in retreat from Wana on 30.5.1919.
Churchill, C. H. M.	Lieutenant	Appointed to Regiment 23.3.1910. Proceeded with the Battalion on Field Service. M.E.F. from 12.10.1914. Killed in action on 17.2.1917.
Cowie, J. E., 33rd Punjabis (I.A. on probation)	Lieutenant	Attached to the Battalion for Active Service 9.5.1918. Transferred to 1/66th Punjabis 12.4.1920.
Dale, C. H.	Lieutenant	Joined the Depôt at Jhelum on 17.7.1918. Demobilised 12.11.1919.

Name.	Rank.	Remarks.
Daniell, H. J.	Captain	Proceeded with the Battalion on Active Service 12.10.1914. Appointed Staff Captain 16th Infy. Brigade 22.11.1915. Taken prisoner of war at Kut on 29.4.1916. Died of disease on 19.8.1916.
Danter, T. E., I.A.R.O.	2nd Lieut.	Attached to the Battalion 29.10.1918.
Davis, G. E. P., 106th Pioneers	Major	Joined the Battalion on 17.6.1921 and transferred to 106th Pioneers on 15.2.1922.
Dawson, A. A. F. C. H.	Lieutenant	Transferred for service with the Mewar Bhil Corps, Kharwara (Rajputana) in 1913.
Dening, L. E., 33rd Cavalry	Major	Attached to the Battalion 23.6.1918. Transferred to 2nd Lancers 4.8.1919.
Dodgson, J. S.	Lieutenant	Joined the Depôt at Jhelum on 1.1.1919. Proceeded on 6 months' leave on M.C. on 10.9.1919 and did not rejoin.
Ducat, R.	Major	Proceeded with the Battalion on Active Service M.E.F. 12.10.1914. Killed in action 11.11.1914.
Dunlop, H.	Major	Appointed Commandant of the 44th Marwara Regiment at Ajmer, and left the Regiment on 9.1.1912.
Elliott, P. W.	Major	O.C. Depôt from 12.10.1914 to 16.5.1920. Appointed Recruiting Officer Peshawar 17.5.1920. Transferred to 71/111th Mahars from 24.11.1921.
Ewers, L. F.	Captain	Joined the Battalion from 71st Punjabis on 26.1.1922. Demobilised on 13.7.1922.

Name.	Rank.	Remarks.
Finnis, B. H.	Captain	Proceeded with the Battalion on Active Service M.E.F. 12.10.1914. Wounded 28.9.1915. Invalided to India 21.10.1915. Rejoined the Battalion M.E.F. 27.1.1916. Invalided to India 9.1.1917 and transferred to 2/55th Cook's Rifles in 1917.
FitzGibbon, L. B., I.A.R.O.	Lieutenant	Attached to the Battalion for Active Service M.E.F. 27.4.1916. Invalided to India 21.1.1918.
Fleming, T., I.A.R.O.	Lieutenant	Joined the Battalion Depôt at Ferozepore, 1916, and served on F.S. M.E.F. 27.7.1916 to 27.12.1919. Mentioned in Despatches 12 . 10 . 1917. E.E.F. 28.12.1917 to 20.4.1920.
Fordham, W. M.	Major	Proceeded with the Battalion on Active Service M.E.F. 12.10.1914. Wounded 17.11.1914. Invalided to India 1915. Rejoined the Battalion M.E.F. 12.4.1916 to 27.12.1917. Promoted Lieut.-Colonel 27.4.1916. E.E.F. 28.12.1917. Appointed Commandant 22.1.1918. Appointed Offg. A.A. and Q.M.G. 3rd Division. E.E.F. July, 1919.
Frith, J. G., 126th Baluchis	Lieutenant	Attached to the Battalion for Active Service 11.12.1918. Struck off the strength of the Battalion 19.11.1919.
Furminger, H. J., M.C.	Captain	Joined the Battalion from 2/26th Punjabis on 1.1.1922. Demobilised on 15.7.1922.
Gardner, R. G.	Lieutenant	Transferred to 28th Punjabis May, 1910.

Name.	Rank.	Remarks.
Hadaway, J. C. S.	Lieutenant	Joined the Battalion on Active Service E.E.F. 16.3.1918 to 20.4.1920.
Harry, F. L.	Captain	Joined the Depôt at Jhelum in 1918 and transferred to I.A.O.C. on 2.12.1922.
Hart, J. H. B. B., 40th Pathans	2nd-Lieut.	Attached to the Battalion for Active Service M.E.F. 20.3.1917. Invalided to India 6.6.1917.
Hawes, C. M.	Captain	Proceeded with the Battalion on Active Service M.E.F. 12.10.1914 to 6.9.1916. Rejoined the Battalion M.E.F. 9.4.1917. Awarded Order of the White Eagle 5th Class (with Swords) by H.M. the King of Serbia. Promoted Acting Major 21.5.1917. Appointed G.S.O. III 17th Division from 12.9.1917. Appointed Brigade Major 7th Infy. Brigade 21.1.1918. E.E.F. 3.4.1918 to 20.4.1920. Awarded D.S.O. and mention in Despatches 1919, Appointed G.S.O. III H.Q. E.E.F. Cairo 2.6.1919. Appointed Offg. Commandant 3.8.1919.
Hawkes, L. V. C.	Captain	Joined the Battalion on 4.8.1921.
Hayes, L., I.A.R.O.	Lieutenant	Joined the Battalion in 1915. Served on F.S. M.E.F. from 10.1.1916 to 27.12.1917. Awarded M.C. 21.4.1917 and E.E.F. from 28.12.1917 to 16.9.1918. Demobilised 1922.
Hensley, F. K., 2nd Guides Infantry	Major	Attached to the Battalion for Active Service 5.7.1919. Transferred to his own Unit 5.8.1919.

82 APPENDICES

Name.	Rank.	Remarks.
Hillier, V. F.	Captain	Joined the Depôt at Jhelum on 7.6.1917. Demobilised on 25.4.1919.
Hodgkins, N. F., 80th Carnatic Infantry	Lieutenant	Attached to the Battalion for Active Service M.E.F. 5.2.1917 to 27.12.1917. E.E.F. 28.12.1917 transferred to 3/152nd Punjabis in the field on 25.5.1918.
Hornsby, R. W.	Major	Posted to the Battalion on 24.11.1921 and joined the Battalion on 9.11.1922.
Hughes, F. L.	Major	Seconded with the South Waziristan Militia in 1913. Killed in action at Sarwekai on 2.3.1917.
Hunter, J., 71st Punjabis, I.A.R.O.	Lieutenant	Attached to the Battalion for Active Service E.E.F. 27.4.1918 to 20.4.1920. Demobilised 1922.
Irwin, E. C.	Captain	Proceeded with the Battalion on Active Service M.E.F. 12.10.1914. Transferred to East Africa to serve with 40th Pathans 5.4.1916. Killed in action 19.7.1918.
Jones, J. L.	Lieutenant	Joined the Battalion on 15.6.1922. Demobilised 24.10.1922.
Keats, A. W.	Lieutenant	Joined the Depôt at Jhelum on 3.11.1918. Demobilised 16.9.1919.
Kidd, G. R.	Lieutenant	Joined the Depôt at Ferozepore in 1916. Served on Field Service M.E.F. 27.7.1916 to 27.12.1917. E.E.F. 28.12.1917 to 20.4.1920. Adjutant 1.1.1918 to 31.12.1921. Mentioned in Despatches 1919.

Name.	Rank.	Remarks.
Langley, L. C.	Lieutenant	Joined the Depôt at Jhelum on 4.6.1918. Demobilised in July, 1920.
Lawrence, R. H. Le M.	Lieutenant	Joined the Depôt at Jhelum on 5.2.1920, from Wellington, India.
Mackenzie, C. F.	Captain	Joined the Battalion from 2/21st Punjabis on 21.3.1922.
McCleverty, P. H.	Captain	Proceeded with the Battalion on Active Service M.E.F. 12.10.1914. Wounded 17.11.1914 and 28.9.1915. Invalided to India 11.1.1917. Attached to 3/9th Bhopal Infantry in 1917. Rejoined the Battalion 1.7.1921. Appointed Commandant 4.11.1922.
McKerron, P. A. B.	Lieutenant	Joined the Depôt at Jhelum on 8.12.1917. Demobilised 1.2.1919.
Messum, L. R.	Captain	Posted to the Battalion 24.11.1921.
Morton-Marshall, F. W., 130th Baluchis	Captain	Attached to the Battalion for Active Service M.E.F. from 27.6.1916. Invalided India 25.5.1917.
Murray, P.	Lieutenant	Joined the Depôt at Jhelum in 1919. Transferred to 1/152nd Punjabis on 23.11.1919. Killed in action on the Frontier in 1919.
Naismith, W. N., I.A.R.O.	2nd-Lieut.	Attached the Battalion for Active Service 5.5.1918. Struck off the strength of the Battalion 22.10.1918.
O'Sullivan, E. T., 66th Punjabis	Lieutenant	Attached to the Battalion for Active Service. M.E.F. 14.5.1917 to 27.12.1917. E.E.F. 27.12.1917 to 20.4.1920. Demobilised 1922.

Name.	Rank.	Remarks.
Palmer, J. H. G., O.B.E.	Major	Joined the Battalion on 10.7.1921 and transferred to 24th Punjabis on 15.1.1922.
Pignon, H. L.	Lieutenant	Joined the Depôt at Jhelum on 10.10.1918. Transferred to Depôt 1/21st Punjabis in 1920.
Pilkington, F. O.	Lieutenant	Joined the Depot at Jhelum on 29.4.1919. Attached to 1/151st Sikh Infantry from 26.3.1920 to 16.5.1921. Demobilised 1922.
Power, W. A., I.A.R.O.	Lieutenant	Attached to the Battalion 13.11.1917.
Price, C. J.	Lieutenant	Attached to the Battalion for Active Service E.E.F. 20.8.1918 to 20.4.1920. Demobilised 1922.
Raper, C. F., I.A.R.O.	2nd-Lieut.	Attached to the Battalion 4.9.1918 and transferred to 1/73rd Infantry April, 1919.
Raschen, G. H., 26th Punjabis	Lieutenant	Attached to the Battalion for Active Service. M.E.F. 7.3.1917. Invalided to India 5.5.1917.
Rattray, C.	Major	Joined the Battalion at Jhelum in 1914 from 26th Punjabis. Served with the Battalion from 22.1.1914, F.S., M.E.F. 12.10.1914 to 16.7.1915. Commandant from 22.1.1914 to 21.1.1918.
Roan, W., I.A.R.O.	2nd-Lieut.	Attached to the Battalion for Active Service M.E.F. 10.1.1917 to 26.2.1917 and from 11.10.1917. Transferred to the Railway Department in Mesopotamia 24.1.1918.
Robertson, R. H.	Lieutenant	Joined the Depôt at Jhelum on 10.10.1918. Demobilised on 3.4.1919.

Name.	Rank.	Remarks.
Rome, H. C.	Captain	Attached to 129th Baluchis for Active Service in France. Killed in action at Givenchy La Basse 20.12.1914.
Rust, N. A., I.A.R.O.	2nd-Lieut.	Attached to the Battalion 19.2.1917.
Saxton, P. D.	Captain	Proceeded with the Battalion on Active Service M.E.F. 12.10.1914. Wounded 17.11.1914. Invalided to India 1915. Invalided out of service 24.1.1923.
Sheehan, M. J. A.	Captain	Joined the Depôt at Jhelum on 26.10.1919.
Stewart, C. C.	Captain	Served with the Battalion on Active Service M.E.F. 18.5.1915. Appointed Staff Captain 16th Infy. Brigade 11.9.1915. Killed in action 22.11.1915.
Stiven, R., 66th Punjabis	Lieutenant	Attached to the Battalion for Active Service 7.8.1918. Invalided to U.K. 12.8.1919.
St. John, R. S.	Major	Proceeded with the Battalion on Active Service M.E.F. 12.10.1914. Wounded 17.11.1914. Appointed A.Q.M.G. L. of C. Basra 8.3.1916. Returned to India 8.6.1917, appointed Embarkation Commandant, Bombay.
Strover, W. G., 5th Infantry	Captain	Attached to the Battalion for Active Service M.E.F. 30.4.1917. Returned to India to rejoin his Unit 16.3.1918.
Swash, N. B.	2nd-Lieut.	Joined the Battalion 7.3.1922.
Tighe, S. M.	Major	Retired from the service 30.8.1913.
Tilfer, A. F., 2/56th Rifles	Lieutenant	Attached to the Battalion for Active Service 9.5.1918. Transferred to 59th Rifles 3.8.1918.

Name.	Rank	Remarks.
Tweedy, H. R. F.	2nd-Lieut.	Attached to the Battalion 4.11.1917 and transferred to 1/89th Punjabis in 1918.
Upton, E. R. B., I.A.R.O.	Lieutenant	Attached to the Battalion for Active Service E.E.F. 27.4.1918 to 20.4.1920. Demobilised 1922.
Walker, H. R. O., 25th Punjabis	Captain	Attached to the Battalion for Active Service M.E.F. 3.9.1917 to 27.12.1917. E.E.F. 28.12.1917 to 8.10.1919. Appointed Bde. Major 233rd Infy. Brigade and struck off the strength of the Battalion 8.10.1919.
Webber, C. D. (I.A. on probation)	Lieutenant	Attached to the Battalion 14.1.1918.
Williams, P. M., I.A.R.O.	2nd-Lieut.	Attached to the Battalion 28.11.1918.

www.ingramcontent.com/pod-product-compliance
Lightning Source LLC
Chambersburg PA
CBHW030401100426
42812CB00028B/2794/J